Joan Armatrading

A Biography

Joan Armatrading
A Biography

Sean Mayes

WEIDENFELD AND NICOLSON
LONDON

To Rikki – *you took me dancing...*

First published in Great Britain in 1990 by
Weidenfeld and Nicolson Limited,
91 Clapham High Street, London SW4 7TA.

British Library Cataloguing-in-Publication Data is available
for this book.

ISBN 0 297 81058 8

Printed in Great Britain by Butler & Tanner Ltd
Frome and London

Contents

List of illustrations   vi

Acknowledgements   viii

Introduction   x

1   I came in this world alone   1

2   A girl for laughs   10

3   Whatever's for us   16

4   Steppin' out   31

5   Join the boys   48

6   With a little dedication   56

7   Oh the feeling   66

8   Light up if you're feeling happy   75

9   Keep on pushing   83

10   All the way from America   98

11   When I get it right   106

12   Right on target   116

13   I write it down in invisible ink   125

14   Take it from me   140

15   All a woman needs   148

Postscript   161

Chronology   164

Discography   171

Main index   175

Title index   179

Illustrations

Between pages 52 & 53

Joan and Pam Nestor on tour in *Hair* (Kimi Wong)
Early publicity shot of Joan (Pictorial Press Ltd.)
The house in Basseterre, St. Kitts, where Joan was born (Joy Fitz-
    Simmons)
Programme for the national tour of *Hair* in 1969
Members of the cast of *Hair* (Kimi Wong)
Pam Nestor and Richard O'Brien, from the *Hair* programme
'*Hair* cast get a West End welcome – in B'ham' (*Birmingham Post and
    Mail*)
Early publicity photo of Joan (Pictorial Press Ltd)
Joan and Pam Nestor with Sumiko (Derek Davies)
Joan in performance (Geoff Swaine London Features International Ltd)
Canterbury Cross School, Birmingham (Sean Mayes)
Joan in performance (London Features International Ltd)
Pam Nestor and Joan (Derek Davies)
Pam Nestor's single 'Hiding and Seeking (No More)' (Chrysalis Records
    Ltd)
Joan in performance (Pictorial Press Ltd and London Features Inter-
    national Ltd)
Joan with drummer Kenny Jones (Richard Young/Rex Features Ltd)

Between pages 116 & 117

Portrait of Joan (David Hill/London Features International Ltd)
Joan on stage (London Features International Ltd)
Front cover of *Sounds*, 25 December 1976

ILLUSTRATIONS

Front cover of *What's On*, 13 June 1980
Joan and her comics (Jamie Morgan)
Publicity photos of Joan (Ebet Roberts/London Features International Ltd and David Montgomery)
Joan at home (Annie Liebovitz/A&M Records)
Front page of *Black Echoes*, 22 October 1977
Joan in performance (Geoff Swaine/London Features International Ltd)
Joan meets the fans, New York, 1980 (Lynn Goldsmith Inc./Rex Features Ltd)
Melody Maker, 18 September 1976 and 16 July 1978
Joan, relaxed (Richard Young/Rex Features Ltd)
Joan on stage (London Features International Ltd)
Joan at New York Pier, 1984 (Chuck Pulin/Pictorial Press Ltd)

Acknowledgements

I should like to thank the following musicians, producers and Joan's collaborators for allowing me to interview them at length – this book would have been impossible without their generous co-operation:

Adrian Belew, Gerry Conway, Thomas Dolby, Jerry Donahue, Anton Fig, Pete Gage, Richard Gottehrer, Steve Greetham, Mike Howlett, Jimmy Jewell, Jamie Lane, Steve Lillywhite, Dave Markee, Dave Mattacks, Ron Mathewson, Pearl Mogotsi, Philip Palmer, Colin Pincott, June Semper, Henry Spinetti, Larry Steele, Liza Strike (Steele) and Kimi Wong.

Thanks to Gus Dudgeon for an interesting evening ... but no permission to use any of his information about Joan (but the Paul McCartney story is his).

I should also like to thank the following people, most of whom are my friends, for their practical help and advice:

David Ainscough, Carlos Alomar, Monica Beadle, Martin Beaton, Neil Brown, Susannah Bruce, Paul Cummings, Sue DeGrande, Geoff Felix, John Lovatt, Joy Mayes (my mother), Yasmin Pettigrew, Jeff Pike, Carol Tierney (BBC Data Enquiries) and Simon Woods.

I should particularly like to thank Pam Nestor, Kevin Cann for his generous help with the photographs and layout, Martin Corteel (my original editor), Stephen Bourne for his invaluable research and help, James MacCall of *The Democrat* (St Kitts) for help at a distance, and

Rikki Beadle-Blair for his detailed advice, encouragement, and the original suggestion for the book.

Much information, all quoted reviews and most of Joan's words came from articles by the following journalists:

Mick Brown, Peter Burton, Barry Cain, Barbara Charone, Ray Coleman, Richard Cook, Caroline Coon, Robin Denselow, Francis Donnelly, Nicholas Fisher, Paul Gambaccini, Sheryll Garrett, Lynn Hanna, Mary Harron, Peter Harvey, David Hepworth, Stuart Hoggard, Peter Holt, Jan Iles, Colin Irwin, Derek Jewell, Robin Katz, Nick Kent, Sue Lawley, Graham Lock, Janice Long, Tim Lott, Austin John Marshall, Chris May, Mark Plummer, Ian Pye, David Sinclair, Robin Stam, Phil Sutcliffe, Chris Thomas, Penny Valentine, Johnny Waller, Chris Welch and Richard Williams – to all of whom I offer my thanks.

Their articles and other information came from the following publications:

The Birmingham Post & Mail, *Black Echoes*, *Black Music & Jazz review*, *Cineaste*, *The Democrat* (St Kitts), the *Evening Standard*, *Gay Times*, the *Guardian*, *Guitar Magazine*, *Melody Maker*, *National Rock Star*, *New Illustrated Rock Handbook* (Salamander Books), *New Musical Express*, the *Observer Magazine*, *Q* magazine, *Radio Times*, *Record Mirror*, *Soundmaker*, *Sounds*, the *Sunday Telegraph Magazine*, the *Sunday Times Magazine*, *The Times*, *Tracks*, *Track Record* (video), *The Voice*, *What's On In London*, *Women In Rock* (Mirror Books)

and agencies: The British Press Library at Colindale, BBC Radio One, BBC Radio Four, The New York Radio Registry.

Joan Armatrading's record company is A&M Records Ltd, 136 New King's Road, London SW6; tel: 071–736 3311.

Joan and Pam Nestor's original record company is Cube Records, Suite 2.07 Plaza, 535 King's Road, London sw10 0sz; tel: 071–823 3773

Joan has no fan club, but her management runs an information service: Running Dog Management Ltd, 27 Queensdale Place, London w11 4sq

Introduction

Over the years Joan Armatrading has produced albums of never-failing inspiration and quality. Her LPs go gold, her concerts sell out and her songs – such as 'Love And Affection', 'Willow' and 'Drop The Pilot' – have become lasting anthems.

There is courage in Joan's writing and courage in the way she has changed from a shy, nervous performer into the confident star with a radiant smile who inspired love and affection from seventy thousand people at the Nelson Mandela concert. She is a guitarist of breathtaking originality, and a singer whose voice goes straight for the heart. Her songs show both vulnerability and great personal strength, intimate yet universal. Short on 'he' and 'she' but long on 'you' and 'me', they appeal to both sexes equally, saying the things we should like to be able to say, but with greater perception, sensitivity and poetry than most of us can ever hope to command.

What is the source of this understanding? Were these songs wrought from intense personal experience? Here the smile fades, the shutters come down. Joan is simply not telling.

This is the first biography of this enigmatic and fascinating star. Joan Armatrading is not, it must be said, the easiest subject. 'Joan Armourplating' – 'the Greta Garbo of pop' – Joan is the most reclusive and secretive of individuals. The book was nearly called 'A Very Private Person', but during the course of interviewing people I heard the phrase so many times it became a cliché. It was no surprise when I contacted Joan's manager to hear, 'Joan feels it is too early in her career for a biography.'

How do you write a book about someone who is so anxious to keep her private life private? Especially when you respect the artist and her desire for privacy? Well, I am a musician, not a journalist, and here lies the answer. In several of her more awkward interviews in the seventies Joan ended up saying, 'You kept asking me questions about myself – you should have asked about my music.' So I have asked about the music. I couldn't ask Joan herself, but I have asked the musicians and producers who recorded and toured with her. All creative artists reveal themselves in their work, and they also reveal themselves to those who work with them.

Pam Nestor was Joan's first collaborator, meeting her on the national tour of the rock musical *Hair*. This raunchy show was an odd début for someone as shy as Joan, but – 'I didn't take my clothes off, 'n' it was great.' After the tour they worked together in London, Pam writing lyrics and Joan the music for their first album – then Pam was fired before the first gig.

Joan has worked with the world's top musicians – not always famous, but invariably talented. They are also generally intelligent, articulate and have a sense of humour. This was important when working with Joan as she could be extremely difficult – but then she also enjoyed a good joke. These people who have recorded with her, toured with her, performed with her, give a vivid and often amusing picture of the strange character and personality of this shy but deter-mined woman. We see Joan arriving at the studio with her songs in pieces, and walking out of a recording session without even letting the producer know. We hear of the 'bullshit' tape which proved Joan was almost impossible to work with. We learn how she started out wanting to be a songwriter, not a performer, and of the row which changed her mind. Joan has always won the respect of musicians, but they have been, by turns, amazed at her raw genius, baffled by her rudeness, impressed with her dignity and warmed by her smile. A fascinating picture emerges of Joan's development – the ugly duckling growing up to be a swan.

Even at the height of Joan's success, with *Me Myself I* at number five in the album charts, her record company turned down an experimental album she recorded in New York. Finally Joan built her own studio and can now record with her pick of the world's musicians, but she is still so private that no one is given the address, and so shy of singing in front of fellow musicians that she would whisper the vocal of a song into the ear of her guitarist!

For her childhood I have let Joan speak for herself. With sensitive interviewers – usually women – Joan has been surprisingly forthcoming about this difficult period of her life. We can see how her isolation produced self-reliance, but also a lack of trust, two threads which run through many of her songs.

Joan is 'a very private person', and her reticence about her personal relationships, may be partly the reason for that. It is reflected in her songs and obliquely hinted at in interviews. She 'feels it is too early in her career for a biography'. With respect – and affection – this book should prove her wrong.

ONE

I came in this world alone

'I don't remember very much about my early childhood ... except my grandmother telling me to kick everybody. And I didn't have to wear a cardigan. And running along the railway track once and splitting my lip, I can remember that! And dressing up in my brother's clothes, me and a friend – not in the same clothes, y'know – and going and raiding the cane field.'

Sugar cane is the main crop on the island of St Kitts in the eastern Caribbean. Joan Armatrading was born in a rough, two-bedroom house in Basseterre, the capital of St Kitts, on Saturday, 9 December 1950. Her parents were Amos Ezekiel and Beryl Agatha Armatrading, née Benjamin, and they had two sons, Joan's older brothers.

When Joan was three her parents went to Britain, taking her brothers but leaving Joan with her grandparents on the nearby island of Antigua. It was not uncommon among West Indian families for people to divide their time between Britain and the Caribbean in their search for work, leaving children in the care of the extended family. All too often this scars the child with a sense of not belonging either to people or to place. Joan was to remain separated from her parents for four years.

'My father came to England first and then I suppose he had to work and save up for everybody bit by bit. So then my mother came and then they sent for me.

'I remember coming to England, all on my own in a big aeroplane with the stewardess looking after me all the way, and I had one of those signs on my neck hanging from a piece of string, saying my name and flight number and so on. And whenever I go on planes and I see little kids like that, it makes me think of me. All I could think of was getting to my parents, especially after such a long journey on my own at seven years old. I'd said goodbye to the people I knew and I'd never been on a plane before. I can remember getting off the plane, and getting on a bus and getting to New Street [Birmingham] – not New Street station, but there was a little hut there where the bus goes to.

'When I saw my mom she was crying and I was crying. I remember that really well! I had two big sties under my eyes and I remember my mum being very upset that I wasn't as well as I should have been. And just being very happy to see her. And not long after that – I don't remember the exact month, but I know it wasn't long after that, I saw snow – which was brilliant! I thought, "Gawd, what's this?" Never seen it before. And I was just in it – I loved it!'

She had been four long years away from her family, and it soon dawned that they were all strangers to her. 'I didn't know my father. And my mother – well, I couldn't remember her at all. And I couldn't remember my brothers either. They'd all grown up, hadn't they!' Her childhood produced a strong feeling of isolation, something which would later suffuse her songs and which is probably the main theme which finds an echo in so many hearts.

'I don't feel as if there are many people I can trust. I had a weird childhood, and that's probably been the strongest influence on my character. But I can't tell you about it because it's not very nice. There isn't a nice way of explaining it, and anyway, I couldn't be bothered to say it in a nice way. It's to do with my parents.'

This is, understandably, something Joan is not keen to talk about.

'If I answer that question I'll have to tell you something about myself. But all right, I was on my own a lot. That's about it, really. I didn't get too involved with the family.'

She didn't get too involved with anyone. 'Took me quite a while to get used to people. When I was younger, growing up, I did a lot of things on my own – going to the pictures, riding my bike, anything I wanted to do I tended to do on my own. I didn't have a bunch of friends. I was an observer. I'd always be the one standing in the playground looking at everybody else playing. It didn't bother me – I was very happy.'

So she grew up in Birmingham – 'Well, that must be one of the most meaningless places in Britain.' At first the whole family shared a single room at 22 Coralie Street.

'We lived in a funny place called Brookfields. It was like a little place all on its own ... a bit away from the centre of Birmingham.' It was a quiet neighbourhood, and predominantly white.

'This might sound terrible, but when I went to Handsworth as a child for the first time, I was quite shocked because that's all you see – a whole stack of black guys. I was used to seeing white guys too. I'd never heard a lot of black guys talk the way they do, and at first I couldn't understand them because it's not the way my parents spoke. My parents never – they didn't say, well, Joan, you're black and those guys are white – have you noticed? It was never a big issue, and it was pretty normal.'

Her father had been a carpenter on St Kitts, but now he was a bus driver. They never seemed to have enough money and the family was still growing. Jacqueline was born in 1960, Tony in 1961 and Andrew in 1963.

In due course Joan went to Canterbury Cross, the local secondary school for girls. She enjoyed school, though she was was quiet and not a typical child – 'I can't swim, I can't skate, I didn't do any of the things I was supposed to do. But I did play the recorder a bit and sang in the choir.' She was often absent from school when her mother was ill, looking after her younger brothers and sister. As the older sister, she was expected to do the housework and look after the home. Unlike her two older brothers who were 'Birmingham ravers', Joan never went to parties or local clubs and she didn't really get to hear much of what other teenagers were listening to.

'The stuff I grew up with was whatever was played on the radio and whatever my parents and older brothers played, which was from Sarah Vaughan and Nat King Cole to Jim Reeves to classical stuff. My family didn't play lots of reggae. In fact, because it wasn't played on the radio I hadn't really heard reggae properly until I did a few gigs in Handsworth. One of my older brothers used to like soul, but I never listened to that, and I didn't get into Aretha Franklin, James Brown and all those until much later on.

'I say I started at fourteen – it might be a little bit earlier – and I started because of my mother getting a piano. She wanted a piano, we had the posh sitting room – we used to live in one room. There was me, my mum, my dad, my four brothers and my sister, we all lived in one room. And then two families moved out, so we got that whole house, and that was when my mum got the piano – to put in the posh front room that we'd never had before. Nobody was playing it, it was just a bit of furniture, she thought it would look nice – which it did. And I just started to play it, and I just made up little bits of tunes and stuff. I didn't start out by learning things that I knew or pop songs and things like that. They had to be things I'd composed myself, however simple.'

She was inspired to write her first real song when she saw Marianne Faithful singing on television. 'I wrote a song for her, but I was too young to know how to get it to her. I can't remember the tune but I've still got those words and the song was called "When I Was Young" – a bit dumb cos I was probably about fourteen or so! Apart from that – which is me talking about being young – the songs were pretty much as they are today: generally about other people. There'd be songs about my school mates or stuff I'd seen on the telly.' Even then, she claims, she would very rarely write about her own feelings.

'I remember that I just wanted to write songs and get someone else to sing them. That's all I ever thought about. That was my attitude even after the first album.'

Joan only had one music lesson in her life. 'When I started to play, just fooling around, my parents said I was good and should have lessons, and so they sent me to this woman and I had one lesson. She taught me E–G–B–D–F–A ... and then she died the next week! That was pretty drastic on my part, wasn't it? She *was* an old lady though.'

Joan's father was an amateur musician. 'According to my mum – most of my information is from my mum – he was a double-bass player in a band on the island' (St Kitts). He didn't encourage Joan's interest in music, but unintentionally introduced her to the instrument which became her first love.

'My dad owned a guitar. He used to sit on the step and play stuff like "Blue Moon", sort of a jazz style, which sounded great, but it was always the same ones! So he's got these two tunes and he'd sometimes hum along to them himself but I never joined in ... I think maybe hearing him made me want to play, so I started picking away when he was out at work. But he didn't want me to play his guitar, so when he was finished playing his bit, he'd hide it – we had this huge room ... we called it "the cellar" but it was actually at the side of the house. It had heavy banklike doors too strong for me to open, if he'd close them well. He used to put it in that room on the high shelf. So I thought, "Well, I'll get my own." And I did.

'I saw a guitar in a pawn shop and I said to my mum, could I have it? It was £3, so I went and told my mum and she said, "Well, I haven't got £3 but I've got two prams ..." so I swopped them for the guitar! And taught myself. That's how I got my first guitar.' Now of course Joan has a large collection of guitars but she has always kept this memento of the happier side of her childhood.

'Growing up, I just spent most of my time playing my guitar or the piano, writing songs. I'd go to the pictures, but generally alone. My two brothers didn't want to play with me – they didn't wanna *gurl* around. When you go to the pictures on your own and you ride your bike on your own, you tend to learn to rely on yourself. I didn't have lots of friends even then. I'd go to the park and walk about, stuff like that – most of the time on my own. But I was very happy. It wasn't a lonely sort of thing.'

This self-sufficient teenager had little musical encouragement at home.

'It sounds terrible when I listen to myself saying this! – but they weren't particularly interested. I was talking about this to my mum about two years ago and she was saying, "We didn't even know you were writing songs to that extent!" They knew I was writing songs but they didn't really know how much I was doing and how interested I was. .... I didn't tell them what I wanted to do or what I was doing, and they probably just didn't think that I'd want to get into something like that. They probably just saw me and my guitar-playing and my piano-playing as just my little hobby – "That's what she does when she's not doing her housework or whatever work she's got to do...." But now, yes, they're very proud, very pleased – very happy about it.'

There was always an uneasy tension between Mr Armatrading and his self-possessed daughter. One night when she was fifteen he threw her out of the house. 'It was the damndest thing. He was trying to fix the telly when I made a silly remark and he just blew his top, telling me to pack my bags.' So into her satchel went a few school books, a collection of limericks she had written and a camera. 'I've never been able to fathom out to this day why I took a camera with me in the satchel.' It is all too easy to imagine the ambivalent emotions which fought in her heart as she closed the door – the mixture of vulnerability and determination.

'Leaving that night was my escape – escape from all those household chores. I was one of six children and I seemed to spend most of my early life looking after my younger brothers and sister. I slowly began to realize that I couldn't remain locked away inside some family cell forever. I needed to get out and the argument I had with my dad that night gave me the key.'

She went to live with her brother's girlfriend, but inevitably her parents begged her to return home. 'They kept on and on until I finally did. But when I walked through those doors I knew I wouldn't be able to last out for very long.'

At school Joan had been working to get the qualifications to become a secretary in a solicitor's office, but at sixteen she had to abandon this ambition, leave school and take a job as the family needed the extra income. She took a job working a comptometer machine in an office – 'but I didn't see myself doing that for very long.

'I used to take my guitar to work and play in the breaks. The boss heard me, and one day he asked me to teach his daughter how to play – which was silly because I was only learning myself. But I said OK, and we got quite pally after that. But the boss under him, who was in charge of our section, didn't like it. She had this thing going, and she told me she was going to give me the sack. So I left.

'I didn't go back to work. I just played the guitar and wrote. Always more into melodies. I didn't used to like the lyrics I wrote. Then it was all stuff about growing up. I've forgotten most of them. My mum probably has them locked away somewhere though. She keeps everything. But I didn't think it was what I really wanted to do until I'd finished *Back To The Night*.'

Eventually she did her first public performance. 'That was some time in the sixties again, and my brother had something to do with putting on a concert at the Birmingham University. He asked me if I would sing a song, which I did, but the only songs I knew were my songs, and he said, "Well, the people don't know your songs, I think you should sing something that they know," and I chose to sing something by Bob Dylan and Simon and Garfunkel, which I think was "The Sound Of Silence", I'm not absolutely sure. And it went down all right. I wasn't the top person on the show.'

There followed 'a couple of appearances in Birmingham clubs, and a talent contest in which I came second. A man playing the musical saw came first.' This led to further small gigs and she formed a duo with a schoolfriend, Scott. For the next year she played bass and rhythm guitar in small local folk and rock clubs, mostly soul stuff, but she didn't really enjoy playing other people's songs. 'It got boring. The guy I was playing with in all those clubs refused to do anything else, though, so I left to work on my own after a year.'

Then Joan had a break which would at last free her from home. 'A guy asked me to go along and watch him do an audition, and while I was there I was persuaded to audition as well. I got the job and he didn't.'

'The job' was to take Joan out of Birmingham, away from her family, and to start her on the path that would lead to her later career. This job was a part in the 'tribal rock' musical *Hair*, which was doing so well at the Shaftesbury Theatre in London that the producer, Robert Stigwood, decided to run a national touring company at the same time. The Stigwood Organization tended to choose a proportion of black and Asian actors for their musical productions and used the Afro Asian Caribbean Agency to find suitable candidates for auditions. This agency was run from Hammer House in Wardour Street, Soho, by Pearl (Nunez) Mogotsi and her husband Edric Connor. They used to advertise in *Melody Maker* and *The Stage* then hold auditions, hiring halls with pianos up and down the country. They were looking for young hopefuls who could move, dance and sing. Inevitably most were completely inexperienced, never having seen the inside of a drama school or dance studio. But some had talent and enthusiasm and a tremendous desire to succeed in one area where colour might be less of a barrier.

Joan arrived with Scott and one of her older brothers. Like many of the girls, she had her hair cut very short and wore dungarees. She sang and played guitar and was gauche, boyish, naïve, shy – but obviously very, very talented. Pearl signed Joan to the agency at about £30 per week and brought her to London where she stayed in cheap digs. Pearl's partner June Semper (sister of actress Nina Baden-Semper) groomed Joan and the others for their audition with the Stigwood Organization.

Joan passed her audition, and the next stage was working with a coach and with Galt McDermott, who wrote the music for *Hair*. She was given one song – 'What A Piece Of Work Is Man', a free-style ballad with words loosely borrowed from *Hamlet*, set almost like a psalm with the music following the vagaries of the asymetrical text. (The odd bars of 3/4 and 2/4 resemble some of Joan's early songs, which were effectively poetry set to music.) She also went on occasionally as one of the 'Supremes', a three-girl group in blonde wigs and blue dresses who, as they go through their stylized Motown choreography, turn out to be wearing just the one enormous dress! They sing the provocative praises of 'White Boys'. Apart from these two spots she was simply part of 'The Tribe'.

Joan soon found herself back in Birmingham, where the show ran for six weeks, then toured major cities for the next year. She has usually avoided referring to *Hair* if she can – in the quote above it's 'the job'. Generally in telling her life story she simply omits it, saying she 'lived in' Manchester and Bristol etc., before moving to London. If asked directly all she says – to everybody – is, 'I enjoyed it, I didn't take my clothes off, 'n' it was great.'

Kimi Wong, a stalwart who had moved to the national touring company from the original West End show, sometimes duetted on harmonies with Joan in 'What A Piece Of Work Is Man'. She remembers that, as an understudy, Joan also occasionally had to recite the 'Abraham Lincoln' speech, with great trepidation but – 'she did it brilliantly'. During some of the backstage boredom, Kimi introduced Joan to the delights of *The Beano*, which started a lifelong interest in comics.

Joan Armatrading did not make her name in *Hair*. Maybe she made little impression. The experience certainly didn't lead her into the world of musical theatre. The wild, uninhibited style and ethos of the show were a far cry from Joan's quiet, reserved character. But Joan met one girl in the cast who seemed to personify all that *Hair* stood for. She was lively and irrepressibly outspoken. She had fronted various semi-pro soul bands in London and already at nineteen was a seasoned smoker and unmarried mother. She had been born just eight hundred miles from Joan, in Guyana on the north-east coast of South America. Her name was Pam Nestor, and she was going to write the lyrics for their first album and give Joan the courage to do the impossible.

TWO

A girl for laughs

Pam Nestor was pretty and petite, two and a half years older than Joan, but with an infectious bubbling personality that must have made the serious, more sturdily built Joan seem older. She was born in Berbice, Guyana, on 28 April 1948. Guyana is a South American country a little smaller than Great Britain. Berbice is a country area, and the main thing Pam remembers about it is the heat, which she loved. She also won a school poetry competition – 'But it's not because I read a lot or anything like that.' Like Joan, her family background was fairly disjointed.

'I didn't have a father around much – I knew my father but just a little. I was brought up by my aunt. We were a huge family really – her family, brothers and sisters.' But again like Joan, she experienced the wrench of a family split, and ended up in Muswell Hill, north London, at the age of fourteen with her mother and her little sister.

'I think for me it was a really drastic change. I should have been brought over here when I was eighteen, perhaps. It was a very strange time psychologically. It was freezing cold! And I didn't understand a word anyone said for ages! I knew they were all speaking English and everything, but it was just a different way of feeling – and expressions.

'Everything that I've learnt or I've written about has been about learning on the street, not in school. All of my boyfriends after a certain age were white. Their attitudes were really secretive, everything was hidden, everything you had to decipher. It's very English – which I didn't know at the time.'

'But the lord above/ He knows that you lie/ And your false complexion's/ Just another alibi.' ('Mean Old Man' – *Whatever's For Us*.)

'Nobody ever gives a straight answer, nobody who's English. And also it's very hard, you have to hide a lot. You know, I say what I feel – and sometimes it's considered to be without diplomacy, but that's just the way I am.'

At sixteen Pam was fronting semi-pro soul bands and three years later she was the unmarried mother of two children. 'Their father's mother brought them up mostly. I was running around trying to be a pop star.' Pam auditioned and joined the first national tour of *Hair* as the show, with its 'shock-horror' reputation, stormed through the provinces. What people talked about was the scene where the cast appeared naked, but this was more hype than reality.

'*Hair* was great – it was really wild!' Pam recalls. 'They loved it! They had full houses and we were stars. It's difficult to tell how good the show really was because you were right in the middle of it and people were being shocked, but I mean – the nude scene was absolutely nothing, really. The whole place was already dark and there were just silhouettes of people. You just got up from under the sheet, sit up really straight for half a second, then there's the blackout! It was like, *big deal!*'

Pam revelled in the show and the lifestyle and feels that's where her hippy philosophy first took root. 'We were all very young and carefree. I mean there were always a few people who were withdrawn like Joan was, but there were others who were just as wild as the show was supposed to be. It was good fun.

'But Joan was not like part of the circle. She kept herself well closed, and every time you saw her she was hugging her guitar. There were few people who were allowed to be in her company.

'The first connection that we had as personalities, we shared digs – six people – I was trying to remember what town it was, but I can't – and Joan used to go down to the basement and play the piano. One day I went down and I was listening to what she was playing. It was good stuff, so I showed her a poem of mine and presto! – a song!'

Joan remembers, 'We shared digs with a lot of people and one night they'd all gone out to a party; so there we were on our own and Pam had some lyrics she'd written, which she passed on to me and said, "Do you like it?" sort of stuff. Well, I was messing about with a tune so I put the words to it and that was "Darkness", the first song we wrote.'

'I was writing poetry really,' says Pam. 'Just rough, and she'd turn it into songs. Sometimes I'd just write endlessly, and she could pull out the essence of it – she did have an eye for that.'

'I can't honestly say I became aware of how to use words till I met Pam. We never actually said, "Yeah, we'll work together." It just gradually turned out that way.'

'At the time I was very prolific,' says Pam. 'Give me a word and I could write about it. And Joan, give her a lyric and she could put music to it. It was that sort of relationship. When we started writing Joan dropped most of the lyrics that she was doing. She did write some songs, but not many. We wrote about a hundred, a hundred and twenty songs. We were partners for three years.'

'Pam used to write a lot of poetry. I could have written alone and some of the album things I did write the words as well as the music, but really I'd rather write with someone else, and Pam is brilliant at lyrics. I did some really crappy words for instance on "King's Garden". I'm not very partial to my own words and "My Family" took me more than a week to finally get down. Most of the time Pam and I work separately. It's very rare that she's around when I'm writing the music to her lyrics. I think we'd argue too much.'

During a hectic year on the road in an endless succession of cheap digs and dressing rooms they wrote songs together – swopping music and lyrics and spending a lot of time just laughing.

'It was like yin and yang, really,' says Pam. 'I was just extrovert – the freak. Joan was introvert. I wouldn't say she wasn't an emotional person, because you can tell by the expression of a song.'

Joan was still in touch with Pearl Mogotsi and the Afro Asian Caribbean Agency, and while she was on tour she caught the train down to London to discuss a publishing contract for the songs. Later she also approached the Noel Gay Organization in Denmark Street (tin-pan alley), but nothing came of this. Pearl and her husband were very easy about their protégés moving on, aware that the agency hadn't the scope to handle the career of a really successful artist.

When the tour ended, Joan naturally moved down to London and she and Pam became involved when six of the cast decided to form a group.

'Me and Joan did original stuff,' says Pam. 'When we joined this "family", Joan played guitar and we both sang, and everybody else tried to do their thing. Not a band really, it was like a six-piece singing/pretend-dancing corps. Was it three males and three females? Something like that. It was called Dice. It was also black and white! That didn't last very long. We only did like one gig. It didn't work out – the whole thing collapsed.'

At the time Pam shared a house off Ladbroke Grove with another member of Dice, Judy Powell. Joan took a room in West Hampstead with friends: 'I had my own room and spent a lot of time there writing, and they understood that. I need to be on my own.' Years later Joan said, 'I do have one good friend, though. I'd do anything for her because she was so good to me when I first started out in the business. She let me stay at her flat. My income was six quid a week then – my rent was five pounds. But I didn't want for anything.'

After Dice Joan and Pam were part of a loose collection of musicians and singers, including Henry Spinetti, who played drums for Joan later and who lived around the corner from her in West Hampstead. Through Judy Powell they met Liza Steele, who sang with Judy, and Liza's husband Larry, who had played bass for Cat Stevens for a couple of years, recording and touring, and also worked with John Lennon and Elton John among others. He later played bass on the first album and in Joan's first band. Liza, who later became a successful session singer, used to make curries when friends dropped in – Joan liked spicy food. But Joan was still so shy that Pam would often have to answer for her, even to as simple a question as, 'Would you like some curry?'

Joan and Pam never shared a flat, but they were constantly together. Joan was still cripplingly shy, and this shyness often came across as extreme coldness, even rudeness, particularly with men, whereas Pam was always losing her head and her heart.

'I remember one time, yet again I was all screwed up over some guy and I came back home and Joan was almost like a disapproving mother, you know – saying, sort of, "Well, I hope it'll be the last time."

'Because Joan didn't like men. I don't know if she still doesn't like them, but men had the most horrific time with her. My boyfriends – the thing about it is that people who are cold – they'll say "Hello", but Joan, you can knock on the door – "Come in" – and she would just look at them, turn her back and watch television all the time, or bang around upstairs. She would do that to some women as well, if she didn't like their character. So, yes, she did open up to me, we were very good friends. I was probably at the time one of her closest personal friends. But she was still quite detached from most people.'

Some of the songs Joan and Pam wrote at this time found their way on to the first LP, *Whatever's For Us*, but in 1971 a recording contract was still a year away. As Joan commented in an early interview, 'It's very hard to convince some people that you are working when you're not being paid. Pam and I worked very hard on the music and the songs for this album, preparing it for nearly two years and never presenting what we were doing until we were convinced it was the best we could do.

'When we had finally finished "My Family" we felt sufficiently confident to make some tapes and take them to people. They weren't easy for people to assess because they were us and people said it was "different" – they had no yardsticks to compare it with.'

At this stage they were hoping for a publishing contract as song-writers. Looking back to that time on BBC's *Desert Island Discs* (1988) when Sue Lawley suggested, 'You didn't really intend to be a performer?' Joan agreed, 'Yes, that would have been brilliant. If I could have written songs and just have people record them, and they say, "That's a brilliant song," and they say, "Who wrote that?" and they say, "Joan Armatrading" – yeah, brilliant!'

So they recorded the songs, not in a studio as a demo to impress a record company with their performing prowess, but on a tape recorder in a flat with Joan strumming guitar or thumping the piano. It was just a rough outline of a song which might catch the ear of a singer or producer – for a professional performer who needed a song and would rearrange it as something of their own.

Doing the rounds of publishers, with Pam doing all the hustling, they caught the ear of somebody at Essex Music – and had their tape accepted. The titles went into the catalogue – and the tape ended up on a shelf in a corridor. The idea was that if someone came looking for a song for, say, Shirley Bassey or Cliff Richard, the agent there would be able to say, 'Yes, I've got just the thing,' and pull it off the shelf. The problem with this method is that in a large publishers no one knows what all the stock is. In due course the person who first heard the tape left the company and from that point no one knew what an Armatrading-Nestor song sounded like. The tape collected dust.

THREE

Whatever's for us

At Essex Music there was a long corridor lined with shelves, ceiling to floor, with thousands and thousands of acetates (demo records) and tapes of songs. One day Paul McCartney came in looking for a song for a new protégée, Mary Hopkin. As the unfortunate assistant was soon obviously lost, Paul picked up a book of titles and out of frustration said, 'Well, let me have a look myself!' He was taken with the title 'Those Were The Days', so after half an hour of searching the assistant played him the acetate. 'Brilliant!' said Paul. 'I'll use it.' In due course Mary Hopkin took the song to number one.

This incident shook the powers-that-be at Essex Music and they realized it was high time they reorganized their catalogue. Mike Noble was enlisted to undertake this massive task. He had come over from South Africa and drifted into the music business. In due course he came upon a tape by Pam Nestor and someone with the curious name of Joan Armatrading. There were four songs including 'All The King's Gardens', strange, raw, folk-inspired pieces which were not the kind of material likely to be covered by a chart artist looking for a hit. It was odd that anyone had given these two a publishing contract. But the voice was immediately striking and Mike, intrigued, took the tape along to Gus Dudgeon, whose office was further along that same corridor.

Gus was one of the 'happening' producers at this time, his greatest success being with Elton John. He had come a long way from tea-boy at Olympic Studios, becoming a good engineer, and was now incredibly choosey whom he recorded. He produced the Strawbs, Audience, John Mayall, Eric Clapton, David Bowie, John Kongos, Ralph McTell and Mike Cooper as well as Elton John. John Kongos was also from South Africa, a friend of Mike, and he had just had a couple of hits on Gus's Fly label.

Gus had formed a production company, Tuesday Productions, with the specific intention of finding new artists to record. He was immediately taken with Joan's raw, deep voice. He was also intrigued by the title 'All The King's Gardens' which was where he had been living in West Hampstead. Joan had spotted the sign from a bus and tried to write a song about it, then she said to Pam, 'Write me a song about All The King's Gardens' – 'and I did,' says Pam.

No one at Essex could tell Gus or Mike anything about Joan Armatrading, so they got in touch and invited her in. Joan and Pam both went along to the meeting. Joan sat with her head down and hardly uttered a word, but Pam was very keen, wanting to know what their interest implied and where it would all lead. She was quick with both questions and answers. Gus and Mike were a little taken aback by the relative personalities of this curious duo, but after several more meetings Gus decided he wanted to record Joan.

Before the first session Joan bought a new guitar, borrowing the money from Lucy Fenwick, a friend from *Hair* and Dice.

Gus was uncertain how well Joan would manage in a studio, so first of all he booked a demo session in London's Marquee Studios, above the famous club in Wardour Street. He wanted to see how these folk-style songs would work with a rhythm section, and called up a couple of Elton John's musicians – Caleb Quaye on electric guitar and Roger Pope on drums – who joined Joan and her friend Larry Steele on bass. It was a difficult session because Joan was entirely self-taught, and the chords she played, the tuning of the guitar, and perhaps most difficult of all, her rhythms and irregular bar lines were a serious problem for even these experienced players. But Gus was convinced that Joan had a very special talent and decided to go ahead and record an album.

Gus had been using Strawberry Studios at the Château d'Herouville, thirty miles south of Paris. He was due to record there with Elton John soon – the *Honky Château* album – and decided to go over a couple of weeks early with Joan and Pam. This time the line-up was Elton's Davey Johnstone and Ray Cooper on guitar and percussion, Larry Steele again on bass and Gerry Conway, who had also played for Cat Stevens, on drums. They all travelled out by van.

Strawberry was 'a gorgeous place', Gerry recalls. 'It was the most beautiful building – traditional French château, quite off the beaten track. It was one of the first live-in studios, owned by a middle-aged Frenchman who was obviously considerably wealthy. He had this gorgeous girlfriend, about eighteen – and everyone used to stare all the time. It was communal eating, French style, very nice!'

The studio itself was upstairs and 'it looked like a big banqueting hall. I think it had a huge wooden chandelier in the top of it. Square drum-booth, beautifully done – the whole place was exotic. And standard type control room.

'The joy of going to a place like the Château – a live-in thing – is that you can settle into an album. You can wake up and go in the morning before anybody else comes in, have a little jam or something, and all these things develop – which is great!'

They got down to work straight away, with Joan playing each song on guitar or piano while the musicians grouped around her and tried to figure out chords, count bars, tap out rhythms, make notes. 'It really was a matter of crowding round listening to a song and then giving a performance with everybody playing - at a simple level,' says Gerry. 'In those days it was very much hit and miss – if the guitarist made a mistake – do it again!'

The way these songs were recorded seems perfectly natural – to anyone unfamiliar with the curious ritual of the recording studio. But since the early seventies, when Joan was making her first album, things have rarely been that simple. Recordings are 'assembled' from their constituent parts, often with some of the musicians who play on a record never actually meeting one another – never being in the same studio at the same time.

It is interesting to note that every producer who has worked with Joan has adopted the same basic strategy: find a band of suitable musicians, allow them to work with Joan to produce an arrangement, then record the result as a 'live' performance. ('Suitable' in this context means brilliant – but sympathetic!)

'She was quite quiet,' says drummer Gerry Conway. 'We'd lean in to hear what was going on! She was very, very pleasant, but I think she was probably nervous and shy – first time in a studio, and all that. But in *my* recollection she's always had an underlying thing that deep down she knew what she was after. But having the courage in those days to say, "Well, you do this and...."' He laughs. 'She did need to speak up a bit!'

So this combination of four pro musicians and one untutored novice blended into a band who could take each seed of a song and breathe new life into it.

'Everybody liked the songs,' says Gerry, 'because she didn't write the norm. The changes were where you *didn't* expect them to happen. It was difficult to learn the material, and not only to learn it but to put in a performance on it and make it sound like you belonged to it. So it was challenging and it was unique. When she started playing guitar – well, people have to put a tag on everything, and in those days everybody said, "It sounds like Steve Stills!" And I suppose it was close to that. She had that ... masculine approach to playing acoustic guitar.'

It was a strange experience for Joan – stranger than for most people on their first album. One of her main musical influences was Joni Mitchell's early work, and she had it very much in mind that this album – these songs – should be recorded with just a guitar or piano, maybe a string bass, flute, something like that. Yet at the same time she couldn't help but be impressed by these musicians and fascinated at how her songs were developing.

Not all the songs needed the whole band, of course. 'My Family' has Joan on piano and harmonium (a small foot-pumped organ) with acoustic guitar and bass. On 'Visionary Mountains' Joan plays piano with an eerie sitar accompaniment, while 'Whatever's For Us' and 'Child Star' simply remained Joan with her guitar. These arrangements came from discussion and trial right there in the studio. Gerry didn't mind dropping out on drums occasionally. 'You just listen to a song and everybody would add what they could. If somebody felt that they should play, they tried it, and if it didn't work, well, "Thank you" and go and sit down!'

Over the years the musicians who have worked with Joan have generally exhibited this spirit of going for the best result without rivalry or rancour, and Gus Dudgeon guided the process skilfully. 'When he's making records, he tends to mix as he's going along, he paints the picture,' says Gerry. 'So you're not going in, playing to half a track, and then suddenly it appears with the LSO on it, or whatever.... He really does paint!

'He was such a dynamic personality, he will take the bull by the horns and as soon as he gets a glimmer of anything, he thinks, "Oh, that sounds good" – he's gonna take it, and everyone gets swept along on that.'

Whatever their doubts, both Pam and Joan were thrilled to hear their songs coming to life.

'It was exciting,' Pam remembers. 'And Joan was excited – she was very confident, and she was very, very sure of what she was doing. So there's this really internal person that's got this guitar and becomes a being.'

Suddenly in the studio the roles were reversed. Joan found herself in her element, whereas Pam, who was 'not the most confident singer in the world', didn't take to the cold precision of the studio.

'When we were in France, which might have been my opportunity to force myself into singing on the album, it just seemed to make more sense to wrap up and let Joan do that. Because the plan was, we were going to work on stage and there was no fuss about that.

'When we were at Essex putting down the songs, some of the songs I sang and some she sang, but all the songs that were chosen to go on the album were the ones she sang, so I got edged out that way. Which I didn't mind – I also had a heavy paranoia in the studio. And it was the reverse with Joan, she had a complete *yucch* on the stage, and I was a total show-off.

'It was Gus Dudgeon's album. I squabbled a bit about the fact that the songs going on the album were his choice. There were loads of songs. We wrote at least a hundred.' When I was trying to get taken seriously as a singer as well as just being the *lyricist*, Gus Dudgeon brought out this Bernie Taupin album – the awful one with him reading his poems and stuff – and gave it to me, intimating that this was what happened to all lyricists who had designs above their station. At one stage I was told by Gus I didn't *have* to be there, I was just like baggage! Incredible!'

Now, with the situation reversed, Pam turned to her only ally, and confided in Joan, who found herself in the middle and under considerable pressure.

Work went ahead steadily, however, and the only serious hold-ups were technical. 'Château Disaster, it was nicknamed! Had a terrible reputation,' Gerry remembers. 'There never seemed to be a proper engineer on duty. You just had to give up and go and have lunch – which was always good in France!'

Despite these problems, two weeks in France saw most of the album completed and when Gus had finished Elton's album he came back to London and recorded the remaining songs in the Trident and Marquee Studios.

The album opens with 'My Family', Joan's steady piano heralding a raw, declamatory voice. There is a challenge here, injecting the allegory of the lyric with an almost bitter irony which Pam may not have intended. Joan introduces us one by one to a family which is something between a commune and the whole world: 'Say Hello ... to Adam he's from the forest/ And to Jane all day she paints.'

'In writing that,' says Pam, 'my family extends outside of the home, and also that everyone has got a special quality – a very hippy idea! They were not real people – it was a spiritual idea really.'

The only poetry Pam can think of which influenced her is Kipling's 'If', which she still loves. 'I got it along the line back home somewhere. There was that other one, I don't know who wrote it – "You may intend a letter to write". It's all about being able to write stuff down if you can't speak it – "though silent your tongue, you can speak with your pen". It's a poem I got from back home somewhere and it's followed me around a lot – positively and negatively. Positively it helped me to write, but negatively, if I got famous, all my boyfriends can print tons of letters – all my naked emotions!'

A clearer influence for both of them is Joni Mitchell. The title song of her album *Ladies Of The Canyon* provides patterns for 'My Family': 'Trina takes her paints and her threads/ And she weaves a pattern all her own/ Annie bakes her cakes and her breads/ And she gathers flowers for her home/ For her home she gathers flowers.' The repetition here is echoed in 'My Family': 'So I bid you welcome/ Welcome brothers/ Welcome to the fold.' This device crops up continually in Joan's songs, sometimes as a litany, sometimes echoing gospel music, sometimes as a rhythmic vocal effect. Among Pam's lyrics we find it again in 'Gave It A Try' (quoted below) and in 'Child Star': 'You're playing games/ Games with nature/ Games you can't afford to lose.'

After this album Pam and Joan ceased their collaboration, and Joan wrote her own lyrics, so it may seem strange to look for continuity or development. However, there are threads running through Joan's work which seem to start on this album, and this suggests various explanations. After completing this album Joan decided that she could write lyrics, so she may have been influenced by Pam, finding in her style or subject matter a new way of expressing herself. Or she may, in compiling lyrics from Pam's poetry, have fashioned a mood closer to her own personality – just as her brooding voice influences 'My Family'. Pam says that Joan had an eye for pulling the essence out of her poetry.

They also share elements of background, and they grew very close during several years of work and friendship. Pam's lyric 'Visionary Mountains' presents a central preoccupation of Joan's work: 'like answers to questions on life, love, and the longing to survive'. Although their childhoods were very different, both had been disrupted by a change of continent, and they found themselves at odds with their families. Perhaps this produces overlaps which are little more than coincidence.

'Gave It A Try' is about returning home, taking a job, 'Showing consideration/ For my relations'. Repeating to mother, father and brothers – 'I have tried and cried/ Tried it your way/ Now I'll do it my way.' Pam says, 'That was directly related to my family simply because I was the wild one of the bunch really. I was not following the pattern of the typical black family – I was running around with hippies – I was an oddity. They wanted me to be regular and straight, and I wasn't.' The song could equally well refer to Joan returning home after her father had thrown her out, and taking a job to help the family's finances.

'Head Of The Table', Pam reports, 'was about a boyfriend, and although it doesn't say, it deals with black and white issues really. His family were very strictly "white for white".' Needless to say, Pam found herself confronted by the boy's father: 'You find that you're unable to do what you want/ The head of the table is stern and strong.' When Joan sings the song, the irony in her voice suggests she may be thinking of her own father, and in 'Mean Old Man' the lines 'You laugh with your mouth/ But your eyes don't blink' could be straight out of 'Show Some Emotion'.

Whatever the reason, we find both vulnerability – which is not an uncommon subject for women writers – and strength. This is a kind of moral strength – of knowing better, or being sure of your ground. It is reminiscent of the protest songs of the sixties, but it may also echo nagging parental adages: 'Whatever's for us, for us', 'Stop acting, acting like a child' ('Child Star'), 'The lord above he knows that you lie' ('Mean Old Man'), 'The head of the table/ Would bend if you're able/ To prove that you're right/ And he is wrong' ('Head Of The Table'). It is already there in Joan's own lyrics: 'Don't take my word/ Just sit back and you'll see' ('City Girl'). This is not merely the voice of the aggrieved lover, it is Pam/Joan, the mother or older sister – or the lover who knows better because she understands what's going on.

Some of the language has rather an epic tone: 'Say Hello to Jo/ She's a goddess/ And to Paul he is a saint' from 'My Family', and 'All The King's Gardens', 'Visionary Mountains' and the title song. This is probably just a hangover from hippydom, owing more to the spirit of, say, Tolkien, than the Authorized Version. However, as Pam says, 'I can't say I've read the Bible, but you go anywhere in the West Indies and we are ... very heavily indoctrinated.'

One tip Joan may have learnt from Pam is that a song lyric need neither rhyme nor scan:

> You could have made me laugh
> If you stayed
> But you left
> I was more confused
> Than I was before you came
> ('It Could Have Been Better').

The music also harks back to the folk/protest-singers of the sixties – Joni Mitchell, of course, Cat Stevens and even early Dylan. Joan sings louder on her first two albums than the more controlled, close-to-mike intimacy which Glyn Johns introduced on *Joan Armatrading* and the albums that followed. This is the voice in the corner of the bar demanding attention, and it suits these lyrics, which inhabit a less intimate world of the emotions than Joan's later songs.

Is this 'black' music? Well, it is not Motown or Atlantic of course, but the sound of gospel is strongly there in some of the singing and piano playing. Gospel music has clearly influenced many white musicians, not least Elton John, and his sound is clear in 'Spend A Little Time'. Now as Joan was recording with Elton's producer and musicians it would hardly be surprising if the Elton sound didn't creep in here and there. However, on this song the actual vocal line has undeniable echoes, with its pentatonic (five-note folk scale) runs and leaps. Probably Gus and the musicians simply responded to something they recognized.

Perhaps all this amounts to is that in popular music all styles and influences are up for grabs. Certainly Joan, teaching herself as a teenager, developed one of the most original talents and voices around. Whatever the influences, she forged her own style.

The album was set for release that November (1972). (There would be no single release until the following year.) All it needed was a sleeve and a title. Instead of a photo it was decided to commission a painting for the cover – again like Joni Mitchell's albums.

'A Japanese couple came round,' recalls Pam. 'The guy took photographs and the woman did the drawing with fine pens. We sat and talked and she listened to the songs and started doing it. It's a beautiful drawing – much better than the cover as it was matt, not shiny.'

The style is naïve and the picture glows with tropical colours like a Gauguin. It is a dreamlike, pastoral setting with striped trees, huge spotted toadstools and tiny flowers with faces. The scene is crowded with images from the songs – a multi-racial 'My Family', a flying child with a star on the forehead, a 'Mean Old Man' in a bowler with his back turned, 'Alice' with a March Hare. In the distance are 'Visionary Mountains' and an ethereal city. In the foreground, looking back at all this, are Joan and Pam. Pam is reclining on cushions with a gentle smile, barefoot, in loose, brightly patterned clothes. Joan is sitting cross-legged in a deep mauve pullover, jeans and big, black, laced boots, a quizzical expression on her face. Beside her, with an arm draped over her shoulder, is a floppy red doll with bells for hands and feet. 'Joan had a little Father Christmas I gave her a long time ago,' says Pam. 'She used to take it round with her and that's him there, a little mascot.'

The album's title came from one of the songs – *Whatever's For Us*. 'It was a heavy struggle to get it,' says Pam. 'They wanted to call the album *Joan Armatrading* which I thought was absolutely not right. So I had to fight for that.'

The back cover has a photo of Joan and Pam sitting on the floor of Pam's flat in St Luke's Road, W11, leaning against a massive carved sideboard. Again Pam is smiling while Joan looks decidedly cool – though an informal photo taken that day shows both of them with Sumiko, the artist, all grinning broadly. Joan's army-style black boot is right in the foreground – she had insisted her boots be featured. The original album cover opened, the centre-spread being the words of the songs with notes on who plays on them, all handwritten. 'It was around the time when they had the double covers,' Pam recalls, 'and the lyrics were written in the Joni Mitchell one.'

Whatever's For Us was released on Cube Records. This was Tuesday Productions' own independent label, distributed by Philips. On 18 November 1972 they took a full-page ad in *Melody Maker*.

It was doubtful whether a first album by an unknown artist – who had done no gigs – would be picked up in a big way, but Derek Jewell of the *Sunday Times* wrote: 'This country has produced at last from the new generation a black singer of total individuality. Her name, Joan Armatrading, her first album *Whatever's For Us* (produced by Gus Dudgeon) is sizzling.' This was just the break they needed and the review formed the basis of half-page ads in most of the music papers – but surprisingly only *Sounds* reviewed the album.

Penny Valentine wrote: '*Whatever's For Us* is a brilliant, crushing album – the kind of collection that you may have despaired of ever hearing from anyone in England. . . .' (This quote was also subsequently inserted into ads.)

Miss Valentine followed this up with an article/interview in the following issue headed 'Joan: dazed and amazed'.

Joan went along to the interview in an old pair of jeans and paint-spattered pullover, and was munching her way through a sausage roll as she explained, 'Pam really does all the talking – you can never turn her off. I find it quite difficult to express what I mean.' She was reticent about influences. 'I never really listened to reggae. In fact it was only a couple of years ago when I went to a few clubs here that I ever heard it. I can't say anyone really influenced me – I listened to everything, still do. But now, funnily enough, I'm much more influenced, I mean, Van Morrison, for instance, really influences my musical outlook.'

25

The same week in *Melody Maker* Joan did an interview with Mark Plummer, who reported, not surprisingly, 'Her voice is powerful, something like Nina Simone's, but when we met for lunch she turned out to be shy and quiet.' Mark praised the album and commented that it has 'quality' stamped all over it.

The album sold poorly despite the reviews. The final total was two thousand. Joan felt this was due to its limited distribution – often the problem with smaller record companies. 'Pam and I used to go round record shops in the East End asking for it. They never had it. We even tried ordering it but they still couldn't get it.'

With the album out, the next step was live gigs. Joan worried about putting together a band good enough to match the studio musicians, but in the event she didn't do badly. Henry Spinetti and her friend Larry Steele had played drums and bass on the album. When Gerry Conway (drums) had been too busy to do all the London studio sessions, Gus used Henry for 'All The King's Gardens' at Trident Studios.

'I got called in to do that session,' says Henry. 'I did the one track, then, would I like to work with Joan? Yeah, love it. Of course, it's the same old story – she was a new artist, they couldn't pay much.' Henry had come up from Wales to play in John Kongos' band, so he met Mike Noble and Gus. Joan's band was completed by Joe Partridge on guitar, and Pam was to sing, of course.

Joan and Pam were being managed by a triumvirate at Sherry Copeland Artistes, a big London agency. John Sherry, from Bournemouth, ran the agency side and managed his own acts. Miles Copeland, son of Miles Copeland, Senior, who ran various parts of the CIA, was later to become famous as the manager of Police. Mike Stone, another American, completed the trio, and later became Joan's sole manager. They decided to start with a London 'showcase' at Ronnie Scott's, the famous Soho jazz club. Pam Nestor remembers the occasion – she has good reason.

'We were rehearsing, I had two songs. I was singing – "Spend A Little Time" that Joan wrote. I love that song, and it suited my voice as well. Then Mike Noble said, do I have to choose one that Joan wrote? If I had to sing, then I should not sing anything that she wrote the words. I think they could recognize Joan's talent much easier than my own. I was disposable, as far as they could see. I was a bit of a trouble-maker and just had too much influence over Joan.'

For once Pam wasn't quick with the questions. 'I was in love with this guy – insane – everything else was of no importance really. So all that was going on and I wasn't completely aware of it. I think Joan was trying to warn me really that something was coming up. I think the business was working on her at the time. I remember going down the road in Knightsbridge and Joan saying to me, "If we didn't work together, Pam, would you still be my friend?"

'And I said, "*No!* – I wouldn't be your friend! You know how important..."

'She goes, "I can't really talk to you, if you say you're not going to be my friend..."

'So we rehearsed two days – then they sat me down and said, "We think Joan should be on her own, *blah-blah-blah*, cos she did record the songs on her own." So I just said, why don't they give me a chance and see how I go? The night when they were all supposed to come and make the decision I had terrible sound. Two days before Ronnie Scott's I got a phone call from Miles Copeland saying, "That's it." And that was it.

'I got really hysterical about it. Joan came around to see what was wrong. And she went into a state because I'd cut off. She tried to persuade me, she was saying they told her that if I didn't go, she wouldn't get a chance at all, and in six months' time she would be in a position to help me, and I should be patient. I said I didn't need her help.

'So suddenly I wasn't going, because what's the point of going when I was no longer a part of it? So then Joan said she wasn't going either, she was going to follow me about wherever I go, *blah-blah-blah*. And the only way that I got her to go into work – she wouldn't let me out the door – was to say to her, "I'm not gonna be your friend if you don't start singing...!"

'You have to laugh now, but that's how it really was – she flipped. So she went to work and apparently the first week of Ronnie Scott's was really weird. And then I went. I think, I managed to get this guy who I was in love with to come with me – to meet me there. I went as a member of the audience.'

So did Gerry Conway, who played drums on the album. 'I think she was struggling a bit. We'd sit and listen to the set, and everyone said, "Well, she's a great guitar player and sings really well, but she seemed unhappy." There wasn't the show aspect – it was, "What am I doing here?" As if she was a bit confused by it.' Gerry and Larry's 'boss' Cat Stevens came to the gig and talked through much of it, but Gerry remembers Linda Lewis saying things to cheer Joan up. 'It was funny, looking back.'

For Henry, on drums, 'It was quite different – a girl singing with deep tones – Whew! made you turn round.... It was great! Ronnie Scott's was good – a good musical thing really. Joan seemed very nervous. She would never talk to an audience then. I remember I used to sit behind going – *Talk to 'em! Talk to 'em!* Quite funny!'

Joan herself later said, 'I never really enjoyed those couple of weeks because it wasn't the kind of place for my music. There's a big difference between that sort of thing and actually being on the road and travelling.'

But Joan was about to travel. Sherry Copeland Artistes was one of the largest agencies in the country and this enabled them to give their acts support slots with big tours. When José Feliciano came over for a European tour this was felt to be a good opportunity to get Joan and the band played in. It was the usual punishing schedule, as Henry Spinetti remembers.

'It was halls, theatres – about fifteen hundred, two-thousand seaters. There was travelling, travelling and more travelling, and not much sleep and more travelling. I remember one thing that struck me as funny – we'd just got out of a car and we got on this train ... Everybody was a bit depressed. You've just travelled, you've had no sleep and you've got to get in the train now. I don't know what Joan felt like because she was the artiste. She might have been thinking, "I wish you lot would stop moaning because I'm doing it as well." We were sitting there and ... I just looked up and everybody had eye contact, and then this hysterical laughter – I never forget, we were doubled up. And it went on for about half an hour – killing. It was like being high. We weren't, but...'

The following June (1973) Joan's first single was released. This was new material, 'Lonely Lady' coupled with 'Together In Words And Music'. They were both Armatrading-Nestor songs and had been recorded by Gus Dudgeon at Morgan Studios in Willesden. This time Cube took quarter-page ads. Chris Welch reviewed it in *Melody Maker*: 'A mean, menacing sound for Joan and her writing compatriot Pam

Nestor that should see them comfortably take a place in the charts, unless the population develops cloth ears overnight.' Needless to say, the population already had cloth ears and the record sank without trace.

That summer Sherry Copeland Artistes sent Joan off to tour the States. The agency had strong American connections and the first album was released over there on A&M. Miles Copeland's brother Stewart, later to play drums for Police, and with Joan on *The Key*, met her in New York. Joan was to perform solo on the popular folk club circuit. Worried as ever about performing, she even asked Pam Nestor to go with her but Pam had had enough, and another friend was flown out so Joan wouldn't be all alone.

Joan kicked off with a week in a club in the Bronx where all they served was ice-cream. She was supporting a couple of fast-talking comedians and it took her a week to understand their act! She and her friend stayed in a hotel on Times Square, and they used to wander around at midnight, blissfully unaware of the area's dangerous reputation. This is when Joan acquired her love of night people, celebrated on 'Back To The Night'. There were buskers and beggars – many Vietnam veterans with pieces of arms and legs missing. Friendly shop-keepers were surprised at Joan's English accent and would sell the pair things at half price. Her big interests in the States were real Levis and guitars, of course, and the friend thinks Joan bought a Fender bass. It was a hot, steamy, smelly summer and they enjoyed being taken out by A&M to a chilly air-conditioned restaurant. Joan had one problem – promotors would give her flowers, and she suffered from hay fever!

Once on tour Joan flew all over the States, with little time to go sightseeing. She carried a small tape recorder and would write songs in her hotel room. Audiences were off-hand at first, but as Joan became more confident the reactions improved. Management were always nagging Joan to talk to the crowds and to wear more appealing outfits, but Joan dug her heels in. In Los Angeles the hotel had a big sign up saying 'WELCOME JOAN ARMATRADING' and shy Joan was delighted!

Meanwhile Pam too was trying to pick up the pieces. In August 1973 she appeared on BBC TV's *Open Door*, and Austin John Marshall of *New Musical Express* was knocked out. Pam's appearance was arresting, her face radiant under a mop of braids, and her voice was raw and true, vibrant with scary latent power. 'Joan's pretty good.

But Pam's different – more savage – more spaced. Blacker.' When he interviewed her, he noted that she was jittery and suspicious and sounded like she'd had her share of knocks. She described herself as 'crazy, tough, intense, idealistic – a typical Taurean.

'Who do I like? Jagger ... Sly Stone ... Hendrix....

'Since Joan's album came out I've been trying to get my own singing scene together. The *Open Door* appearance has been my first break.'

That week *Open Door*'s subject was the Basement Project, a group of black East End kids who had made a 16mm movie, *Tunde's Film* (with help from Maggie Pinhorn and Alternative Arts). Pam had sung the film's theme song, 'Dinah's Café', which she and Joan wrote, and Joan and Larry Steele (bass) were among the backing musicians. Larry had always encouraged Pam. She was now recording with a band which included Henry Spinetti on drums, and Ken Cumberbach was producing, but it was another six years before Pam could get a single released. It was not in her nature to be bitter, but she had a tough time of it.

'Everything I tried to do after that was clouded with Joan Armatrading – every step. Joan used to say she'd hate to be Elvis Presley's brother. Well, I hate being "the person who used to write with Joan Armatrading" – all it's done is hold me down. I was always being compared with Joan Armatrading although my style is different vocally. But somebody actually said, "We don't want a second Joan Armatrading," so I was never allowed to record.

'We wrote about a hundred, a hundred and twenty songs together, and we were partners for three years. So it's very difficult for me now, because when I write, people say, "This reminds me of Joan Armatrading." But nobody ever thinks that Joan could have been influenced by me at all.

'Every now and then people come up and they say, "Oh, I remember the first album," and that's really nice. But it's not very often, and basically I'm her shadow and I don't like it at all.'

FOUR

Steppin' out

By 1974 Joan was in limbo. *Rolling Stone* had voted her Best Newcomer of 1973, but her album had sold only two thousand and the single failed to chart. Gus Dudgeon, who produced the first album, was out of the picture. He had fallen out with his partner David Katz in Tuesday Productions and the two had parted company. Joan decided she wanted to leave Cube Records, but it took her a year and left her with a debt and no contract. With no records to promote, the gigs dried up and the band drifted apart. Henry Spinetti remembers it all sadly.

'We used to see each other now and again socially which was quite nice – I mean, we were young. Not like now. I remember she came round my flat once and asked me to form a band with her, which was quite touching really, when I think about it. But at the time it was, "I'd love to, but I'm doing these sessions at the moment." You would get asked to play on somebody's album or something, it would be for a lot more money.... It's one of those things, I wish I'd said "Yes". Mind you, maybe a couple of years she might have found another drummer.'

American Mike Stone was now effectively Joan's manager. Tall, thin, affable, with a high-domed forehead, he had a smile which Henry described as 'painted on'. Mike had no other acts so he was naturally very keen to see Joan succeed. Since Pam's departure Joan had been very difficult to handle. Mike wanted to do a deal with A&M Records, but Derek Green, the head of British A&M, had turned her down, feeling she was uncommercial. So Mike Stone took the unusual step of signing her direct to the American company. He flew to Los Angeles and got a deal with Jerry Moss, an old school buddy.

So now Mike had an artist and a record contract. He needed a producer. Mike looked to the agency. Sherry Copeland Artistes was a large stable and within it was a whole assortment of artists, bands and musicians. The name Vinegar Joe means little now, but in the early seventies they were a fine, raw blues band fronted by two singers – Elkie Brooks and Robert Palmer. The guitarist bandleader – and Elkie's husband – was Pete Gage (who had played in The Equals back in the sixties). Pete had recently produced an album for Hustler, another band from Sherry Copeland Artistes, and it had done well, so Mike approached Pete.

Pete Gage knew that Vinegar Joe was soon to be broken up and Elkie and Robert would pursue solo careers. He was going to be involved with Elkie of course, but felt there would be no harm in taking on another job in the meantime. It turned out to be quite a job.

'I was dragged in by Mike Stone who said, "Right, we've got a problem. We've got a very difficult artist but we believe she's got an immense talent – but we're not musicians, we don't really know. Take a listen to her material, see what you think. The songs need a bit of work, she needs a bit of work, but we think there's something there. We don't even know what style it should be in, but it has to be commercial."

'The qualifications necessary were to be a producer-engineer, and arranger-songwriter, somebody who could handle difficult women – my wife, Elkie, was notorious for being difficult, so I had a good background there. They also needed somebody who could hold the reins on money, which was one of the big problems in the initial stages. It was quite complicated, the whole thing.'

Pete, hearing she was signed to A&M in Los Angeles, expected a black soul artist, and it took him a while to find out what he had taken on. He became suspicious when he had to meet four different people before he was allowed to meet Joan herself. He was also told specifically *not* to listen to the first album – 'it'll give you completely the wrong idea.'

As these meetings progressed, he began to realize that confidence in this act was not very high. 'So it was a challenge to me.' And he was keen to do well with an artist who was signed to the A&M label in California.

Derek Green, as head of British A&M, was one of the people Pete met. Derek was in a strange position in that Joan had been signed 'over his head' by the parent company. In an interview years later he reported his own first meeting with Joan. 'She had an inner strength that told me she was going to be a major artist, and I vividly recall her first remark, "You know, I can't eat good reviews." She was worried that she would become a cult artist loved by the media but unknown by the mass public. I replied, "You deliver those songs and we'll sell the records." '

Pete already knew Derek and had been amazed to learn that, as a general rule, he regarded female artists, particularly black female artists, as poor investments for the record company. Now Derek told him that he could see no point in recording Joan. She was totally uncommercial, had no image whatsoever and wasn't a particularly nice person. However, Derek had been instructed by his American bosses to go ahead with the album. 'But money would be tight and I would have to report to him at various stages during the project to let him know how progress was going.'

Pete also heard of an incident with Tony Burfield who was TV promotions person for A&M. When Tony first met Joan he did the show-business thing, grabbed hold of her and gave her a kiss on the cheek. Joan was dreadfully upset and actually ran out of the building. They had to chase down the road to find her.

Mike Stone himself was very anxious about the project as this might be his last chance to succeed as a manager in Britain. Pete found that 'it was no good talking to him on an artistic level. The fact that he had teamed up with Joan still fascinated me. Maybe it's because they had no way they could possibly relate, that they couldn't work out how much they hated each other.' Part of Pete's job was also to try to persuade Joan to change her appearance, her attitude and various other aspects to make her marketable. 'So before I even met Joan I knew we had immense problems.'

Finally Pete heard a tape of Joan's songs, at which point he realized he was dealing with an artist with folk roots, not soul. He went to see her in her West Hampstead flat.

'The Joan that I met was sullen, introverted, totally paranoid, was unable to look me in the face or really carry on any sort of conversation. I think I managed to get through to her in the end by explaining that I was different from the other business animals she had around her, and that possibly this time she'd got a friend, somebody she could relate to.'

Joan had no piano, but played and sang him the songs, strumming vigorously on her acoustic guitar. Here he encountered another problem. 'Each time she did a number it would vary. She was doing complex time changes which first time through I was thinking, well, OK, that bar happens to be 7/8, or 15/16 or whatever. The next time she did it, it would be 5/8 or sometimes it would be straight time.' Pete realized he would have to explain some musical basics if Joan was to work well with other musicians. 'She didn't take particularly kindly to that – she didn't really see why it was relevant.' So Pete explained that she had to work with musicians because this was part of making her more commercial.

Another surprise was that Joan's distinctive chord structures resulted from some highly individual ways of tuning a guitar. Normally Pete could work out the chords a guitarist played by watching the fingers, but when he ran into difficulties and went to try something on her guitar – '*bloing!* – I realized that her tuning combinations were absolutely fascinating, some of them totally illogical.' Joan couldn't explain them to him. 'This is when it dawned on me I'd got somebody with a *huge* amount of natural talent, because at the same time as she was completely undisciplined, the fact that she was attempting it was outrageous. Most people would never have got that far. So the musical spirit, the musical imagination was gi-normous.'

Joan used different tunings for different numbers. 'I use open E and open D, and a sort of open seventh. It's ... I don't know – a strange one.'

'Quite often she used to forget what the tuning was,' says Pete, 'so you'd have to wait ten minutes while she fiddled around. Later on I found out there was Pam Nestor who did exactly the same fucking thing with a piano! What they must have been like together was amazing!'

Pete came away from that meeting thinking hard about the musicians he would need. They would have to be very capable to be able to follow Joan's rhythms and chords, but not top session players because they wouldn't have the patience to deal with such an untutored talent. Pete needed people who would be sympathetic and patient – and maybe it would help if they needed the work!

As part of the process of befriending Joan – 'trying to get through to her that I was a normal human being' – he took her back for a meal with his wife.

'They got on quite well. I thought they would get on *very* well to start with. Elkie is a severe cook – brilliant cook – and because it was Joan and I knew Joan loved hot food, she did some sort of chilli, and it was a hot one! And I'll never forget, Elkie came out, presented the food, and Joan said, "Have you got some pepper sauce to put on this?" – typical Jamaican style – cover everything in pepper sauce. And we turned round and said, "Look Joan, you should try that first because Elkie is no typical English cook. If she makes chilli, that's gonna burn. Check it out." Anyway, "No, no, no, I definitely want some." I think Joan probably lost half a stone when she ate that meal! You could tell she was baking, she didn't know where to put herself! Elkie and I were concealing little laughs because we knew that she totally mis-estimated our Elks there!'

Pete booked a week at Rockfield Studios. This is a rural musicians' 'holiday camp' built around a farm, with houses and chalets in the grounds so bands can hole up there in peace (or mayhem!) – a good place for concentrated work. Pete's plan was to put Joan with a rhythm section and establish a few fundamentals, then work towards finding a commercial direction.

Joan's music 'wasn't folk – there wasn't a musical bag you could put it in. There were little bits of jazz influences, various other things flying around. What I had to do was find out what there was and which way to take it.'

He spent a lot of time with Joan going over and over the songs, working out the various permutations. 'Because every time Joan did a song, some parts would remain the same, while other bits – quite important bits – would drift. Quite often she couldn't make it to the end of a number.'

So Pete painstakingly wrote out various formulas rather than arrangements, particularly for the drummer. Then they could try out different permutations so at the end Joan could turn round and say,

'That's what I mean – yes, that one, not that one.' 'Because I didn't really want to make this decision for her, I wanted to protect her own flow.'

They worked on five songs, mostly piano-based ones. On these first sessions Joan played piano or acoustic guitar. There were three other musicians. John Halsey, from Patto and The Rutles, was the drummer – an invaluable talent. 'He's a great "feel" player, able to understand complex time signatures and just float through them, make them sound like nothing happened, whereas most drummers would sound like they fell over.' Steve York from Vinegar Joe played bass, a moody character, but he ended up quite close to Joan. Colin Pincott was the guitarist, a big, genial man who had played with such diverse talents as Presley and Hendrix.

He remembers, 'She had very strong feelings about the words of the songs. I remember her sitting at the piano narrating certain ideas and things. The thing that struck me at that particular time was that her keyboard voicing for her songs was as strong as her guitar stuff. She had certain voicings a bit like Joni Mitchell, which worked for her alone.

'She just played her tunes so very *strongly*' – and he laughs – 'it was apparent to the musicians what should happen next. But I don't think she was used to musicians going, "Oh, well, this bit needs that – the guitar solo needs this ..." She was a bit taken aback with it. There was one track which called out for an old Strat country solo, and I overheard Joan saying to Pete, "It's too country," and the guy's going, "That's what it needs." And of course afterwards she used guys like Albert Lee because she obviously realized that it did need the country thing.'

Pete, as producer, found himself stuck in the middle of this. 'That first week was absolute hell. Just on a social basis, Joan couldn't handle meeting new people. Everybody would turn round and say, "She is so rude – she's such a horrible person." I could realize, getting to know her a little bit by then, that she was complex but she wasn't malicious. She sounded like she was short-tempered, pissed off, etc. But it was just that she was so paranoid she couldn't relate to other people. I had to spend a lot of my time being diplomatic to people, saying, "Don't rock the boat, just go along with it – yes, I know she shouldn't have said that."' (As Steve Lillywhite says, 'When you first meet Joan she comes across as bloody-minded rather than shy.')

'It's all about the relationship thing and the atmosphere,' says Colin. 'It didn't quite ring true – it didn't knit in. It was very, very close indeed – I think the songs were amazing, she was terrific. But the mixture, the playing didn't quite knit in. The old phrase springs to mind, "tight but loose". This was tight but not loose. Later on – after working with many people – she loosened up, and of course it worked.'

After several days Pete was getting desperate. 'When it did come together Joan was still incapable of singing the whole of the vocal. The guys were becoming more and more frustrated that there was nothing ever to follow.'

Joan would mumble something – 'funny little noises' as Pete puts it. ' "What do you mean?" "Well, I don't like it." "What don't you like about it, Joan?" "I don't know." '

'And that would be as far as you would get. And of course we were starting to tear our hair out by then.'

'There were certain days,' says Colin, 'when the atmosphere got a little bit heavy, and we all, in our own ways – we musos – tried to lighten it. One of the things I said I'm sure Joan would remember with horror. She played an acoustic Ovation, and she was always interested in guitar stuff – she knew I'd jammed with Jimi Hendrix and she wanted to check that out. One day when the atmosphere got a bit worse for wear I remember turning round to Joan and I said, "Joan, Joan" – the atmosphere you could have cut it with a knife – I said, "Joan, stand your guitar on the floor," and she got her Ovation out and stood it there. "Now what have you got?"

' "I don't know." '

' "A standing Ovation!" Of course all the musos fell about! But Joan didn't see the funny side, bless her heart.'

On another occasion, 'One of the songs called for a mandolin effect on guitar, so I used a hairbrush because it gives that certain effect, which is something I've done since I was a youngster. It created that sound and "Great!" she said, "that's it!" – until she saw how I did it. And obviously she thought, Is he taking the mick? Of course I wasn't, being genuine.'

'This is the way it was starting to go,' says Pete. 'I could feel discipline and anybody taking this whole project seriously were fast going out the window. Luckily at that point Joan's girlfriend came down and I gave her the best part of the day off.

'She was much more perky about that. As soon as her friend arrived her personality changed – she was absolutely radiant.' That's the first time he saw the famous smile. 'One of the great appeals of Joan's smile was it was like a ray of sunshine hitting a completely iced planet. That's when I realized that, underneath all the iron façade – the "armourplating" that was her nickname – that she was a wonderful and sensitive ... and humorous person. Because in certain moods she could be great. But it wasn't at this stage that I appreciated that.'

Colin remembers the rare smile. 'There were odd bursts of that – more so when she was away from the piano, because most of the songs she wrote with the keyboard tended to be a bit heavier, a little more melancholy. The lighter songs where you did see her smile were guitar.'

Towards the end of the week things were still no better in the studio, and Pete decided on desperate measures. 'I don't think Joan actually knows about this to this day, but that's when I had to take out my own personal insurance policy. Because at the end of that week I was going to have nothing respectable to play anybody, just a vague sketch. So my insurance policy was to run what I call a "bullshit" tape – you run a full reel of tape all through the session, so you get bits and pieces of the performance, but you also record all the conversations in between. That's what I had to have to be able to prove that the musicians were doing their bit, that I was doing my bit, and the reason we weren't getting anywhere was because of Joan herself.'

Pete came back to London armed with 'a pretty dodgy five tracks and a bullshit tape' and reported to Mike Stone and A&M. He told them, 'There is a tape, if you don't believe me.' But knowing Joan, they did believe him. Derek just wanted to know, 'Well, is there something we can go on?'

Pete said, 'Well, there is. But you've got to give me a little bit more time to get to know her. I'm gonna have to be really hard-faced about this now. I'm gonna have to say, "Right Joan, I've listened to your song: this is how it goes. You don't think it's how it goes, but this is how it goes, because otherwise we won't get anywhere."'

Pete explained that he had listened to all Joan's songs, and her music showed several distinct styles – a strong jazz influence, a folk root which leant slightly towards a reggae/calypso/Caribbean feel, and then there were the up-tempo songs which put him most in mind of Richie Havens, when she got thrashing away. Mike Stone immediately favoured this style as being the most commercial 'so he could get his BBC air-play'.

But Pete suggested he should run with all three styles using three different combinations of musicians, because Joan's music didn't have a single identity. This would make an interesting album from which could be chosen the most likely singles. Folk and jazz based songs had been hits for other people, and although Mike wanted dance grooves it was still doubtful how successfully Joan could move in that direction.

Pete chose one set of strong jazz musicians and another 'black music'/funk-soul combination. The latter was based around Jean Roussel 'one of the finest and most expensive piano players ever to come out of this country! Jean was such a helluva musician and such a helluva personality – once he took a direction *nothing* could stop him. That's partly what I wanted, because if I gave Jean the instruction and said, "Right, I want it to go in this direction," once he'd got the thing down, I knew it was going in that direction and nobody was going to stop it.' Jean could play on all the keyboard tracks as he had both the jazz and funk backgrounds.

Pete booked the next sessions at Island Records' Basing Street Studios, just off Ladbroke Grove, west London. Stevie Winwood and Free recorded here, and it was very central, which was important for Pete as he was busy with other commitments. 'I was just shooting in there, putting down some ideas, spending a lot of money....'

Now that Derek had agreed the funding Pete was delighted to have such a brilliant band and was pleased to be starting this next stage on a high as the Rockfield sessions had been so down. He felt sure Joan would respond when she heard her songs coming to life. However...

'This is mistake number two! Lessons To Be Learnt, by Pete Gage! The earliest session was 'Steppin' Out'. There was Tony Newman, who was with Boxer, had been with Sounds Incorporated for years, white drummer, but at the same time serious funk, James Brown, lay-it-down, he's-got-all-the-grooves man. He and Jean knew each other well. Bernie Holland, certainly one of the finest guitarists in the country – nothing Bernie couldn't play. Phil Chen, who's with Rod Stewart of course, established Jamaican Chinese extract. Gaspar

39

Lawall, one of the forefront *now* of the Afro, New World music. So we had a combination of Mauritius, Africa, Jamaica and added British funk players, all heavyweight players, all charging double rates, you know – expensive guys.

'Joan walks in – she's late, of course, as usual – and they're in there cooking. She's walked straight into the studio, walked straight back into the control room where I'm stood, and gone, "Who are *they?*"!

'And I said, "They're the guys I was telling you about – the greatest guys in the country. You wait till you hear your song – the way these guys are gonna play it, they're gonna play it great!"

'And she says, "Yes, but some of them are black."

'And I didn't know what to do with myself – I just fell about laughing. Because this was just something that I wasn't ready for. And I said, "Joan – what do you mean? You don't want black guys playing on your record?"

'And she said, "Well, I don't suppose it matters really," and wandered back out to the studio.

'Well, that really blew me apart. Now in hindsight, obviously what was going on in that little head at that time was very, very complex.'

While this is undeniable, it is also true that Joan has chosen to work with black musicians both before and since – Larry Steele, Sly Dunbar, Robbie Shakespeare, Manu Katché.

Once she had made her protest Joan was fine. She went back into the studio, the musicians introduced themselves, she was just her normal moody self. But soon there was so much energy coming from the line-up that she couldn't help but respond. Much later she looked back and practically disowned this album because she wasn't in control. But then, as Pete puts it, 'She had no control, she had no direction, and unfortunately it was my job to seize the reins and give her direction and just hope that she liked it.' He was still very careful always to ask, 'Do you like this? Is that OK?' And at this stage – Yes, it was. She was beginning to thaw and enjoy herself – 'she starts to come back into the studio smiling'. It was the happiest time for both Pete and Joan.

A particular success was 'So Good'. Joan played the basic track by herself, then made it quite clear she wanted no other people doing vocal backings – she desperately wanted to be a 'choir'. She probably didn't realize that she would have to sing her parts twenty times! But she was doing it herself, 'so she took to that like a duck to water, and she enjoyed doing it – there was a lot less pressure.

'I think where I cracked it eventually with Joan was when it came to "Dry Land", a very sensitive number, and my favourite number from that album – I loved the song.' They recorded her playing and singing the song four or five times to achieve the best take, but it was done virtually live. 'She played, sang, and that was all there was to it.' Joan was worried when Pete said he wanted to add a little texturing with the synths, but he kept it very simple, and felt he had made progress when Joan asked him to play guitar on one or two numbers. 'She started to respect me as a musician, and life became a bit easier.'

Joan herself said afterwards, 'I was a bit hesitant about having a musician as a producer because they always seem so anxious to play. But Pete worked out well. The thing was, I hadn't done anything for so long and suddenly here I was making an album. I mean, I'm not the type of person that sings willingly anyway! I think everyone expected me to go into the studio and do it perfectly first time around. Whenever I sing I always don't want to.'

Pete soon came up against this last problem – and hit another brick wall. As songs were completed instrumentally Joan would record her final vocals, but she was unhappy because the engineers in the control room could see her through the glass. 'Rod [Thear] was only about seventeen, and he thought Joan was hilarious. He thought it would be a great idea to build her a hut! So he took all the screens and he literally built a hut *including* a sound board on the top! And it had a little entrance way where she went in and all the mikes inside. We were all tickled pink! Joan liked Rod, because being a very young and very open sort of guy, it was quite clear that he didn't mean any malice, and she used it quite happily, no problem.

'But some of the vocals weren't really getting there – she was still mumbling words and singing out of key and didn't seem too happy with things.'

Joan comments, 'I didn't sing very well because I wasn't happy, and I didn't play as well as I could have. There's fault in a lot of areas but I'll always blame myself. If an album is good it's my fault, and if it's bad, it's my fault.'

The vocals were taking far too long and Pete was losing patience. 'At one point – must have been about 9.30, quarter to ten, and we're half-way through a vocal – and Joan just stopped. This wasn't unusual – I'd just get on the intercom and say, "Joan, what's happening?" She'd say, "Oh, I'm thinking about this" or, "I don't like these words" or, "I wanna change that" or, "I don't like how I'm singing that." That was acceptable – quite commonplace.

'This one occasion I got on the intercom and said, "Joan? What's happening?" Nothing, not a word. So – this again wasn't unusual – wait two or three minutes, ask her again. Because maybe she was in a sultry mood. Still nothing. So I said, "Better see what's going on." Walked out, look in the little hut – no Joan. I assumed she'd gone to the loo. All right, give it five minutes – she hadn't turned up. So then I'd gone round, shouted in the loo – "Joan, you there?" Nothing.

'So give it about half an hour, I thought, maybe she's gone out, maybe she's coming back – because she was very independent in her own little way. I went up and checked with security: "Oh no, Joan left, three-quarters of an hour ago." Really!'

Pete was 'leaping mad' and when he got her on the phone he tore her off a strip for being 'so bloody rude. OK, I will accept that you turn round and say, "Well, I'm not happy, I'm in a bad mood, I don't want to sing, I wanna go home." But just to walk out like that and leave us all just hanging there. We're giving you every possible opportunity. Now what is the problem?'

'And she said, "The problem is, I don't want to be a singer."

'I said, "What?"

'She said to me, "I don't want to be a singer."

'I said, "You what?"

'She said, "I don't want to be a singer. I want to be a songwriter, I just want to write songs but I want other people to sing the songs."'

Pete didn't raise the subject again that day. They carried on with the vocals, but it wasn't very fruitful.

'With that album,' Joan said later, 'the reason it was unsatisfactory was more owing to the fact that I just did not get involved in it that much. I'd leave the studio and forget I'd been there. There was simply a lack of involvement on my part. I was just going through a bad period really.'

The next day Joan was going to Reading to see a friend so Pete drove her to Paddington. On the way he read her the riot act.

'I should imagine Joan would remember it, because I shouted and screamed at her, and she just sat there having to take it all in. I explained to her that thousands of other artists would give their limbs to be in her situation, to have a record deal, the musicians involved, the studios – all the facilities that were being offered to her. And for her to now turn round and explain to all these people that believe in her that she doesn't want to be a singer is ridiculous and she's being very, very selfish. And I had a go at her for being childish – everything I could hit her with, and I really thought, this is going to be the make or break between me and Joan. And I said, "You get on that train, and I either never ever want to hear from you again because you've given up the industry, because if that's what you want to do, then give it up. Or, the next time I see you, you'd better bloody well deliver." I didn't mince my words at all.

'And there was a little glimmer of a smile, and a little twinkle in the eye as she left. She still looked pretty serious, but I just saw this little flash as she got out of the car, and I thought, yes, she's gonna come back and she's gonna do it. And this was the essential factor. Somebody had to tell her. Nobody had told her and it befell me to do it. Anyway, then she came back and she was a lot more open, she got on with the job. She'd still have her little moody patches, but then we started to make music.'

This story is obliquely confirmed by a comment Joan made in an interview with Caroline Coon of *Melody Maker* a couple of years later. She was talking about growing up. 'I just played the guitar and wrote. But I didn't think it was what I really wanted to do until I'd finished *Back To The Night*. Doing that album I was really miserable. I thought it was a load of rubbish, a waste of time. Then, as soon as I'd finished it, I couldn't wait to do the next one. I suddenly realized that this was my career and I was going to make the best of it.'

As these later sessions progressed, Joan started to trust Pete, and to rely on him when she had her own doubts about the music. She let him press on and get things finished. He still always asked her, 'Do you like this? Do you like that?' She didn't enjoy the process of mixing very much, so they just used to invite her down towards the end of the mix when things were taking shape. 'And one way and another we completed an album that Joan and I were satisfied was the best thing we could have done at the time.'

Perhaps the session they both enjoyed best – and one of Pete's all-time favourites – was when the double-bass player Ron Mathewson came in. He is a jazzer, one of the top bass players in the country, a veteran of Ronnie Scott's and Humphrey Littleton's bands, and had played with the world's best on their visits to London. For all this, he's a very friendly, unassuming character, with an accent declaring his birthplace on the northern tip of Scotland.

'He just flew in there, blasted away.' Pete had heard of Ron through Elkie, who had worked with Humphrey Littleton. 'I wanted something to complement the acoustic side of Joan – some sort of solo interest going round in addition to what Jean was playing but still to have just this mixture of jazz and folk.'

It's an experience Ron remembers well – his one and only rock session ever.

'When I met her she said, "Hello, nice to meet you – all right?" And they stick me in a corner in a box somewhere. . . .

'When she came in she sat down at the piano right away. She was good – she could play it. The only problem was that she could not relate what she wanted.'

The most difficult but successful track was 'Body To Dust' which was virtually a duet between Joan's voice and Ron's bass. The timing had to be felt rather than counted, but the result was electrifying.

'She wanted to have bass going *do-do-do-do-wah*. I ended up with about ten million chords in different time factors – it drove me mad! She wanted me to have a bass solo. That was with the whole band – it was all percussion stuff and I tore around for a little while. Now I know that tune so well – I even dream about it sometimes.

'Joan was great, I thought, she was lovely. Maybe she was actually a little bit nervous. Well, I got the feeling that she was quite shy, but the same time she knew what she wanted. She didn't actually make a point of saying, "I want this." She was very, very good mannered. She was a lovely person, but that was the hardest gig I'd done for a long time.'

The sound achieved the desired effect, but as Pete says, 'Of course, it added to the lack of identity – the *confusion* around that album. But it was an experimental album and Joan was individually very pleased with all the tracks.'

'No Love For Free' opens with Joan's guitar, cool and clear. Her voice is immediately more controlled and more secretive on this album. Joan takes the part of a hooker, distant and independent. 'There are a lot like you/ They want to save my soul.' But it is not simply strength – there is the inability to accept love – 'I'm flattered/ But I don't understand'.

The album is aptly titled – *Back To The Night* – as many of the songs are about night people and activities. They contrast the night's sin and pleasure with the morning of rebirth and redemption – 'Jesus woke me up in some/ Stranger's bed' from 'No Love For Free', and 'Giving us to the morning dew' from 'Come When You Need Me'. There is also a sense of travelling, and of the prodigal returning to forgiveness and succour – 'Travel So Far', 'Steppin' Out', 'Dry Land', 'Come When You Need Me'. This recalls Joni Mitchell's *Blue*, an album which has obviously inspired and influenced her.

Joan also calls on religious imagery – 'Get In Touch With Jesus', 'Body To Dust' – something which occurs occasionally throughout her work. This does not necessarily suggest any special interest in religion – Joan's views are pretty conventional Christian-background-plus-touch-of-Eastern. But religious imagery is very strong and poetic, an obvious attraction to a songwriter, especially one whose territory is the soul. In 'Get In Touch With Jesus', Jesus becomes a metaphor for the lost lover – 'the man/ Who can help me dream again'. In this song there is also an echo of the pattern of Joni's 'Ladies Of The Canyon' – 'At bevelled mirrors in empty halls/ Empty halls and bevelled mirrors' – in Joan's lines, 'Make my mind blank/ Set my heart free/ Mind that's blank/ And a heart that's free'.

Joan's ambivalence towards her lyrics is clearly shown by two comments she made about a single song. First to Penny Valentine in 1977 she said: 'If you take "Body To Dust" for instance, nobody knows what that song's about. Oh yes, I know what it's about! But that was a song I was trying to write about me, yet I didn't want to tell people so much about myself. So then you try and disguise the fact it's about you, and consequently it comes out where nobody knows what's happening. Now I've got over that a bit – also I can write songs that are practically nothing to do with me and make it seem as though they are!' The second comment about this song was to Paul Gambaccini eleven years later: 'Now I know for a fact that that song is about me – it's about something that I've been through – and I couldn't tell you what it's about. It's so coded, and I'm so busy hiding this thing, that I think, why the heck did I bother to write it? Cos I don't know what it's about. But now I've grown up and know that if I'm gonna be in that position, just don't write the song.'

Two of the songs have Pam Nestor's lyrics – 'Dry Land' and 'Come When You Need Me'. Both of these take the theme of the comfort and protection to be found in returning to a friend/lover, but seen from the two different sides: 'Let me sail to the depths of your soul' and 'This love of mine will comfort you', a poignant reminder perhaps of the bleak side of going it alone – and another slant on *Back To The Night?* Joan later said of the song 'Steppin' Out': 'It was a personal situation which wasn't really doing me any good. I'm not stepping out of emotion as such. I'm just deciding, because of a lot of things around me, that the only sensible thing to do was to be on my own completely.' 'This lady loves/ And she goes where she pleases/ No love for free.'

Musically this album shows a development of the mood of the first album, exploring the different strands of Joan's talent. After the solo opening track, 'Travel So Far' displays a band sound which is immediately more confident than anything on *Whatever's For Us.* As Pete Gage planned, we hear rock, folk, gospel, jazz, blues. The music is diverse, but the album hangs together because of Joan's voice and presence, and the mood of the songs. Later albums were more polished, but the first two still hold their own by the quality of the songwriting and the conviction of performance.

Predictably, perhaps, Pete got two different reactions from A&M. 'I remember Derek Green just looking totally bemused by it. I think it's quite obvious he didn't like Joan as an artist. Jerry Moss came over from the States, came round to Elkie's and my place in Fulham, sat, listened to it, he really did enjoy it. He said it was an adventurous album, that I'd done a good job.

'Mike Stone was very happy, though musically he didn't really know what was good or bad, so he was playing it to other people. He made me remix a few things – which I was quite annoyed about. He wanted *more voice – more voice.* I think we lost a lot, the texture of the backing. It was just the blind leading the exhausted.'

Pete Gage was more than exhausted. Over the six to seven months he had been working with Joan he had come out in a nervous rash – dermatitis. 'I would come home *totally* wound up, disease starting out all over my feet, my elbows are peeling and my hands are falling apart. And Elkie used to say – her exact words – "Why do you work with these fucking amateurs?" '

Once Mike Stone was satisfied with the remixed album he was determined to do everything in his power to make it a hit. So he went straight to Fabio Nicoli, A&M's art director and they decided on Clive Arrowsmith for the photography. 'He was hot property,' as Pete puts it. 'He still is hot property, but then he was red hot – *the* man to use.' Mike, knowing Pete was now on good terms with Joan, asked him to discuss the cover with her.

Joan's reply was characteristic. 'I've thought about this – I don't want any photos. I don't want my picture on the cover of the album. It'll have to show something else.'

Pete reported that back to Mike, 'and Clive Arrowsmith of course found it was hilarious – "Well, how am I gonna photograph somebody who doesn't want their photo ...?" So everybody put their heads together and they came up with the idea to persuade Joan that if it wasn't front face, and on the proviso that you couldn't see her features – that was the main thing, she didn't want her features – that a silhouette would do. So that's what Clive came up with. Which was brilliant – which became her logo. So really on Clive's end, the guy proved his genius. Because I had a bad task, but his task was impossible!'

FIVE

Join the boys

Joan liked the album, Pete Gage liked the album, manager Mike Stone liked the album. The next step was inevitable. Mike called Pete up and said, 'Right, now you are the only person that can relate to Joan, she listens to you, she'll do what you tell her – I want you on the team.' Mike asked him to find Joan a permanent band. 'What we've got to do is get Joan up there, doing her material, and sell her to her own record company.' Another showcase gig at Ronnie Scott's club was the goal, a good classy place to invite record company executives.

Pete felt that if he could find the right band, Joan could relate to them and have the opportunity to develop her music. They would have to be good players, but cheap because Mike didn't have much money. The usual music biz story!

Once again Sherry Copeland Artistes solved the problem. John Sherry had been sent a tape by 'a bunch of university wallahs from Cambridge called The Movies'. Pete went to see the band with John, though not with Joan in mind. 'Walked in – The Movies were brilliant, one of the finest young bands I have ever seen. They were so tight, highly intelligent, entertaining, everything is fabulous about them. I put it to them bluntly, "Look, I know an artist who desperately needs a band. You desperately want to have a record deal, but because your music is not that commercial, nobody's gonna give you a record deal. But how about if I try and work something here where I get you your

48

own album on the condition that you also work with this artist, and you'll also get a subsistence salary?'' '

Jamie Lane, the drummer, takes up the story. 'It was a *fait accompli* really. We heard her stuff and liked it, and thought this was an excellent way to pull the band together, give ourselves something permanent to do and push ourselves forward a bit. Particularly as a record deal of our own was tied in.

'We were doing slightly Latin tinged funk music. We had Durban [Laverde], a Venezuelan bass player. A lot of us had heard and liked Latin music and he showed us what went on, to make it up. In those days we were very influenced by the likes of Steely Dan, and our own backgrounds were sixties, seventies black soul. The band was a mishmash of all these influences. Very rhythm orientated, because we had drums and percussion – Julian Diggle, he's the percussionist.

'When we first started with Joan, Pete Gage was always there acting as an intermediary. Cos there we were, quite a noisy six-piece band, and Joan, sensitive solo artiste – it wasn't an obvious match! Pete acted as communicator. The first thing we did was learn the songs off the record, and adapt them for our band line-up. Pete would ease the whole process, and Joan would either like it or not. And if she liked it, fine, if not, we'd work around it until we came up with something that worked. It was a fairly haphazard process, but it worked well.'

Back To The Night was launched by A&M with a big push. They took the back page of *Sounds* with two paragraphs of slightly pretentious spiel, an approach that became the Armatrading promotion style, just as the silhouette cover-photo became her trademark: 'If you want to know a little about the beautiful side of Black Truth, take a listen to this album ...' etc., and ending: '*It's the truth. Get back to it. Back to the night.*'

They celebrated with a full-scale launch party at London's Playboy Club! *Melody Maker* duly registered the event in their 'Hot Licks' gossip column, impressed with Joan's tasty set, powerful style and mightily swinging new band The Movies, noting that Joan played good guitar too. Faces at the party included Kenny Jones, Chris Jagger and the inevitable bunny girls.

As Pete Gage comments, 'The reason it was the Playboy was purely that Mike [Stone] knew the people there, Victor Lowndes, all the rest of it. It was probably the weirdest place anyone could have chosen for

Joan. But at the time it was just a room where they could do their launch. If I remember rightly, it wasn't particularly good. Joan was a bit introvert as usual.'

In fact it was just too early, as many promotional events are. Joan and the band were not properly played in yet. But first there were reviews and interviews. Barbara Charone, an American writing for *Sounds*, did a glowing in-depth album review. She was not afraid to criticize, but was very positive, saying Joan exhibited 'a maturity missing from her past work. '*Back To The Night* is not a great album but it ... easily promises great things to come ... Her melodies and song constructions have greatly improved ... Joan Armatrading possesses enough talent and variety to make that great album. Who cares if it takes two years?'

Like Penny Valentine before her, she followed this review with an interview the following week. This time Joan announced, 'I'm the most boring person in the world.' Barbara noted that she was still wearing the front door key round her neck. 'I was worried about reviews because I just didn't think anybody would like it cos it's different – for me at least. I'd like to do a whole album that was sorta jazz-bluesy. This album is getting there – you can hear a sorta leaning-towards.' She felt that Pete Gage had more empathy towards her songs than Gus Dudgeon: 'Pete worked out well.' Joan recalled something critic Richard Williams had said at her last Ronnie Scott's appearance – 'What's she doing on stage?' – and felt that this time would be different. 'I'll enjoy the road this time because I've got a band. It's like – before, when we'd go shopping someone would tell me to buy something and I'd buy it even if I knew I'd never wear it. And it was a bit like that on stage. I'd do a number just because someone told me to. But I'm happy all that's changed. I'm hoping I'll be able to get across what's me.'

This time Joan succeeded. The gig that brought it all together was another two-week stint at Ronnie Scott's in August – very different from her début there three years ago. She and the band had been doing some promotional work – *The Old Grey Whistle Test* for BBC TV in May, and then up to Scotland.

Drummer Jamie Lane remembers, 'That was an extraordinary period, because that's when the band was playing at its best. Although poor Durban had been through this horrific train accident. Joan had a radio promotion to do up in Glasgow, live radio broadcast, and some of the band went up by overnight sleeper, which didn't make it – it crashed in Nuneaton. Durban lost his foot in the rail crash. I was in it, Greg was in it, and Dag, the keyboard player at the time, he was in it as well. The rest of us got out of it with cuts, bruises and a bit of concussion, but Durban unfortunately lost his foot. But extraordinary man that he is, he just said, "Right, that's happened – onwards."

'In no time he was out of hospital and we did a month of gigs at Ronnie Scott's. It was the summer of 1975 and the temperatures were just unbelievable. And in a stinking jazz club, there was Durban just out of hospital, playing two sets a night up until three in the morning. He was unbelievable. The band, we were playing really well – I've got great memories of that stint and we got some incredible reviews. A lot of people remember us from that.'

Robin Katz, writing in *Sounds* certainly did: 'Joan Armatrading is like a multi-faceted painting. She ... suggests a tapestry of a dozen designs. Her phrasing stops lyrics half-way through a sentence to let the piano speak ... and the arrangements surround her like a blanket of flowers. ... Her band was one of the most receptive acts of musicians I'd seen in ages.' Joan sounded 'sturdy, committed and very real ... and she makes you remember how refreshing pure music can be when it needs no fancy dress to carry itself.'

On the subject of fancy dress, Robin noted that she was 'clad simply in jeans, a plain shirt and the ever-present house key on a chain round her neck'. This outfit owed something to Pete Gage: 'I'd done an absolute miracle which Mike had asked me to do three months earlier. I had actually got Joan to take off the Blue Sweater. She lived in a big, baggy, blue sweater. The first night at Ronnie Scott's I remember, she was going to wear the Blue Sweater, but I managed to persuade her into wearing a white blouse. She wouldn't remove the key from round her neck, and I said, "That's fine! Cos that's a gimmick!" Mike Stone's attitude was, "Right, she's got a good pair of knockers, why shouldn't people see it?" And I thought, "Jesus, if he says that to Joan..."'

'I've always worn clothes that I feel comfortable in on stage,' Joan explains, 'which means the jeans I've got on now with a blouse or shirt. They kept saying things like, "Have you thought of wearing a dress or putting your hair up? At least stop wearing that little woolly hat on stage." I went right on doing what I wanted to do. You've got to be a bit stubborn because most of the record business is run by men, and men always have set ideas about how things should be. There's a lot of pressure on women to conform. If you want to survive you've got to be either strong or stubborn or deaf.'

Pete feels The Movies were Joan's ideal band. 'They were very good humoured guys, very intelligent, so they were able to handle her ups and downs, they were also very sensitive. By the end of Ronnie Scott's Joan was starting to shine. We did start to see that famous smile – which really was sunshine after the rain.'

Joan and The Movies were now at their peak, and fully ready to go on the road. 'The first tour we did with Joan was us supporting [A&M's] Supertramp,' Jamie remembers, 'so we all piled onto their tour bus. So our introduction to touring was at quite a good level, because all the dates on that tour were the Odeon circuit, so we had decent hotels and decent transport, and the whole thing was really quite cushy.'

Joan sometimes found it strange playing to Supertramp's audience. 'At one venue I looked out and there was no one over twenty. I felt wrong. They wouldn't want to listen to me – though if I was a bloke it would be different. I thought, what do you hear when you hear me? If a young person isn't listening, you expect him to start unwrapping a sweetie!'

After Supertramp they did a tour of the east coast of America. Jamie Lane remembers: 'We played some odd clubs on that particular tour. We did the Bottom Line, New York, which was wonderful – truly excellent. Greenwich Village, it doesn't put on fashion-type acts, it puts on music-type acts of all sorts, from folk to jazz. I remember we got this great stage sound in there. It was really quite uplifting.'

The Movies became very important to Joan, and not just as a backing band. For the first time she found she was part of a musical unit, and as the music drew them together she used them as a medium through which to test new material.

'Some of the gigs we did were really special,' Jamie recalls, 'because in a small place like Ronnie Scott's the effect is enormous – not only on the audience but on the people doing it. It's much greater than if you're doing it at Hammersmith Odeon.

'She did "Dry Land" – just Joan and the piano and a tiny bit of synthesizer from Dag [Small]. "Dry Land" was a single ... And we did "Love And Affection" where three of the band came up to the front

ABOVE LEFT: Joan Armatrading and Pam Nestor during the national tour of *Hair* in 1969.

ABOVE RIGHT: Early photo of Joan.

BELOW: The house in Basseterre, St. Kitts, where Joan was born.

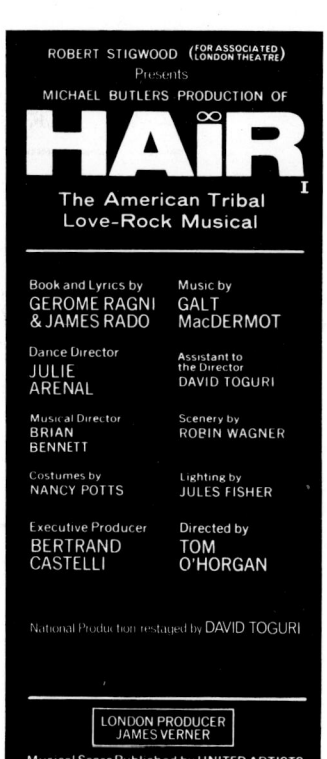

ROBERT STIGWOOD (FOR ASSOCIATED LONDON THEATRE)
Presents
MICHAEL BUTLERS PRODUCTION OF
HAIR
The American Tribal Love-Rock Musical
Book and Lyrics by GEROME RAGNI & JAMES RADO
Music by GALT MacDERMOT
Dance Director JULIE ARENAL
Assistant to the Director DAVID TOGURI
Musical Director BRIAN BENNETT
Scenery by ROBIN WAGNER
Costumes by NANCY POTTS
Lighting by JULES FISHER
Executive Producer BERTRAND CASTELLI
Directed by TOM O'HORGAN
National Production restaged by DAVID TOGURI
LONDON PRODUCER JAMES VERNER
Musical Score Published by UNITED ARTISTS

To MiKE + Helen
Love & Happiness
Always
Kimi

Trevor Sends his love

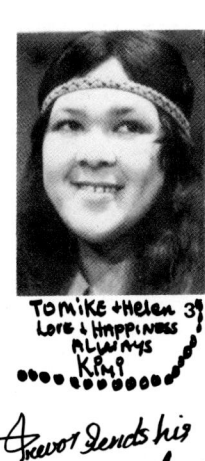

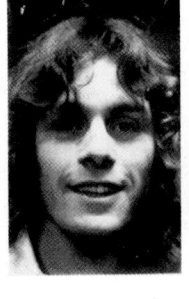

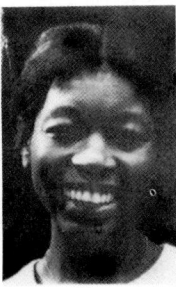

ABOVE: From the tour programme of *Hair* – Trevor Ward (left), Kimi Wong (above left), Paul Nicholas (middle), Floella Benjamin (right).

BELOW: The cast of *Hair* outside the Sheffield Lyceum, with (left) Floella Benjamin and Pam Nestor; (centre) Richard O'Brien and Joan; (top right) Trevor Ward.

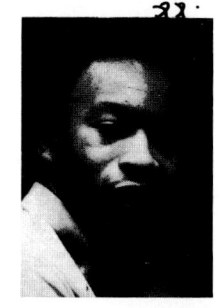

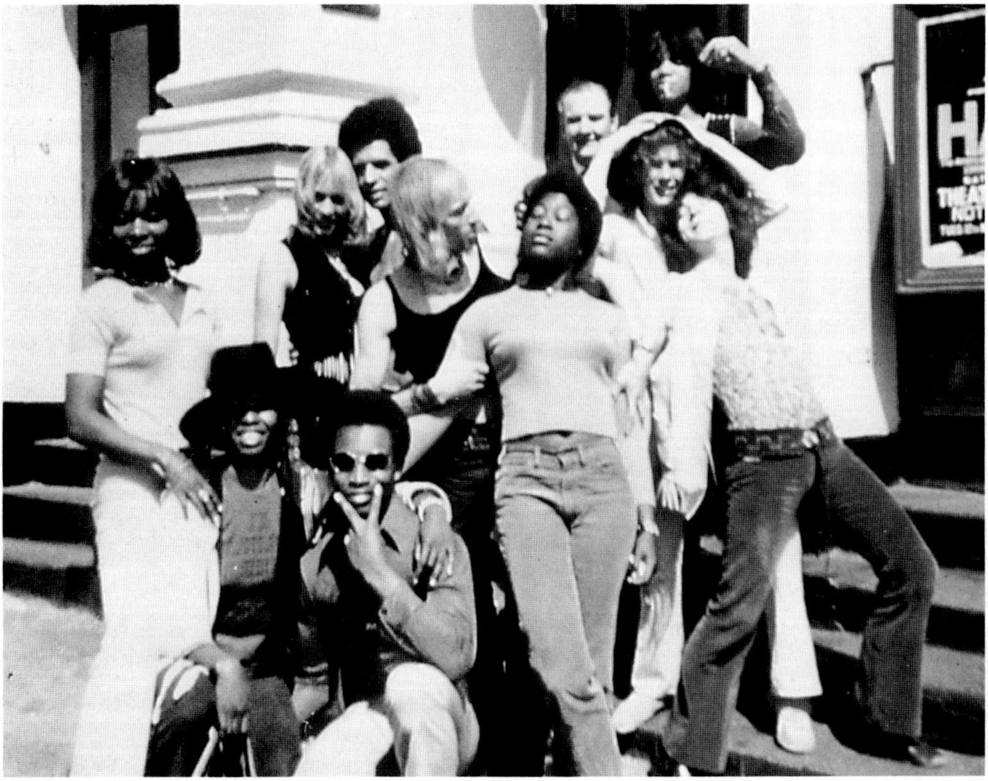

ABOVE: Photograph and article from a Birmingham newspaper, shortly after Joan joined the cast.

BELOW: Promotion for *Hair*: Pam Nestor and Richard O'Brien.

Much love to Mike & Helen
Pamela Nestor

THE LONDON CAST RECORDING OF HAIR IS AVAILABLE ON THE POLYDOR LABEL AND PROJECTS WELL THE GUTS, ENTHUSIASM AND IRONIES OF THIS EXCITING SHOW
ROGER BAKER

.... ON POLYDOR STEREO ALBUM NUMBER 583 043

polydor

Dig it people – the city of love is in sight
Love
Richard O'Brien

'Hair' cast get a West End welcome — in B'ham

by FRED NORRIS

THERE was a "West End welcome" for the company of the hit musical "Hair" when they arrived in Birmingham today — both in terms of personal greetings and in box office receipts.

To meet them as they arrived at the Birmingham Theatre for the final dress rehearsal before tonight's opening performance was Gary Aflalo, one of the starts of the West End production.

His presence made it a Birmingham-London link with a difference.

Gary lives at 6, Elm Grove, Kingshurst, and he met some of the other Birmingham members of the cast. They included Joan Armatrading, of Station Road, Stechford, and Tony Noons, who used to live in Moseley.

Also in the cast is Ziggy Byfield who was born in Redditch.

MARVELLOUS

Mr. James Verner, the show's producer, gave the box office news: "In Birmingham we are certainly in business. The bookings are marvellous."

He added: "There are now three productions of the musical in the United Kingdom. One in London, another which opened in Scotland last Thursday, and now Birmingham tonight.

"This means that on Saturdays, with six performances in various parts of the country, 'Hair' will be breaking new theatre records by taking £10,000 just for one day."

The show is in Birmingham for a six-week season.

There was an error in the all-correct line for the "Hair" contest published on June 12. Picture B was No. 8 and not 10 as stated. The contest was, of course, judged correctly.

ABOVE LEFT: Early publicity photo of Joan.

ABOVE RIGHT: Joan and Pam Nestor with Sumiko, who painted the album cover for *Whatever's For Us*.

ABOVE RIGHT: Joan in performance.

BELOW LEFT AND RIGHT: Canterbury Cross School (now the Broadway
School), Perry Barr, Birmingham.

OPPOSITE: Joan on stage at the Hyde Park Festival, June 1975.

ABOVE: Early publicity photo of Pam Nestor and Joan in Pam's flat, St. Luke's Rd, London W11.

LEFT: Pam Nestor's only single, *Hiding and Seeking* (*No More*), 1979.

ABOVE: Joan in performance.

BELOW: Joan with drummer Kenny Jones who played on *Joan Armatrading* and *Back To The Night*.

and did backing vocals – this was before it was actually recorded and became her first major hit. So we worked on a lot of the songs that were on the *Love And Affection* album.'

'For the first time,' says Pete Gage, 'Joan was writing the shape of a song, taking it along to her musicians, and playing it to them. Consequently Durban Laverde came up with a bass line – *dum, dom dom* – which was the root of "Love And Affection". I realized that we were really onto something so I took down the Revox and taped them. I still have the original rehearsal tapes of "Love And Affection", "Tall In The Saddle", "Change The Water Into Wine" and one or two other tracks.

'I went in to see A&M and said, "Right, we have cracked it – this is it! This is gonna go somewhere." Presented them with the tape – fine, no problem. Yeah, they'd take a listen, and get back to me.'

Mike Noble was the man at A&M who took the tapes – Mike who had first discovered Joan's demo tapes at Essex Music four years ago. He had been following Joan's career closely, and when she moved to A&M, so did he, joining the A&R [Artist & Recording] department.

Pete didn't hear from A&M immediately, which puzzled him.

'What I do discover about two or three weeks later from Mike Stone is that they're gonna go ahead and do a second album, but I would not be required for it. I was obviously very upset by that, and I said, "Why not? I've done all this..."

'"Ah no, A&M have decided they need a name producer for it."

'"Well," I said, "what about the band – what about The Movies?" Because I did care for those guys.

'And he said, "Unfortunately the same thing – our contract with them is going to be finished."'

Pete feels this treatment was really dirty. He and The Movies had done all the work preparing the ground for the successful album that followed. 'The demos had been done for the necessary hit.' And it was worse for the band because their money simply stopped. Joan wasn't available for comment, but this was understandable as she was in no position to take up Pete's case. 'That was between me and Mike Stone. I just took the hard-nosed attitude – Elkie was now entrenched with A&M and her things were starting to take off, so I thought, well, I'm annoyed about it. But of course at that time I didn't know exactly

53

what it was gonna go on to do. It would have been nice – with hindsight!'

Movies' drummer Jamie Lane is even more philosophical about it all: 'I can quite see why we didn't go into the studio with her, but at the same time I'd love to have done it. We must have spent the best part of nine months working together. Glyn Johns was obviously an extremely good choice as producer. He had his circle of musicians, Jerry Donahue, Dave Mattacks, etc., who were all much more experienced, studio-wise, than we were at that stage.

'We had a lot of life and excitement, which they missed, but they had the refinement needed for a record. We were disappointed to be blown out, but it was quite obvious why that happened.'

As Pete Gage says, 'I don't mean to take anything away from Joan insomuch as she had the raw talent. If she hadn't met me and The Movies, maybe it would have been somebody else. Because she certainly has got the ability. But she did need that catalyst to shape her into what she became.'

Joan later said, 'I liked Movies, but they were a band, a self-contained unit within themselves. They had their own things to do. Anyway, I just fancy changing, working with new people as often as possible.'

This account inevitably telescopes many months and much work. As Jamie says, they had a lot of life and excitement. After Ronnie Scott's, Joan and The Movies joined American Nils Lofgren for a Stateside tour, and British group Supertramp on their American and British tours. They did one hundred gigs in as many days, continuing into 1976.

Pete Gage's story has a coda. (In fact it has two, but one comes later.) 'Not very long after that I had a phone call, and was approached by Pam Nestor. As soon as I heard Pam Nestor play – there's one number, it was the blueprint for "Dry Land", there's no doubt about it. I think Joan had actually learnt bits and pieces of Pam's piano playing.

'When I met Pam Nestor and saw the personality, the outgoingness, I suddenly realized what had been happening with Joan – she was only half of the act. With The Movies she had learnt to become herself, she'd found her niche.

'Pam was the pushy one – she was that much more extrovert. She went on to have one reggae hit and loads of children, from what I can understand.'

SIX

With a little dedication

Glyn Johns was one of the major producers of the sixties, working with Joe Cocker, Family, Steve Miller, Led Zeppelin and Traffic. He kicked off the seventies with The Rolling Stones, The Who, and two albums for The Eagles, which he regarded as his best work to date – until he produced *Joan Armatrading*. Glyn was on good terms with Derek Green of A&M. When Derek asked him to produce Joan's next album, Glyn was a shrewd choice. He was not only successful but had an undeniably strong commercial sense. Joan, with her two albums, had achieved considerable critical acclaim on both sides of the Atlantic, but as yet not a sniff of a hit.

At first, though, Glyn was not at all keen on the idea. He heard *Back To The Night* and didn't like it – 'It was a very busy record' – and was puzzled when he saw Joan live. Maybe his interest was caught by the demo tape Joan made with The Movies. Anyway, he finally agreed to the project and first met Joan when she was appearing at the Cellar Door Club, Washington, DC.

'Before we met,' she recalls, 'everybody kept mentioning all the names of the famous people he has produced. But he came up and said, "Hello," just like a normal bloke. He gave me a limp handshake and I thought, "Oh, I like him." He had on sporty clothes and a hat which really suited him, and he looked really nice.' Joan herself was keen on hats at this time as a way of shielding herself from direct gaze.

Glyn knew the musical approach he would need. He had recently produced the *Rising For The Moon* album for Fairport Convention, with Sandy Denny singing, and decided to use musicians from the Fairports as they were used to working in an acoustic context.

Drummer Dave Mattacks is a small, dapper individual, very keen and quick. Guitarist Jerry Donahue, in contrast, is a tall American, with that relaxed way of speaking which belies a clear head and a sure touch. Glyn preferred working in the studio with as 'live' a band set-up as he could contrive. Just as Pete Gage and Gus Dudgeon before him had realized, this was the only way to record Joan. Peter Woods on piano and Dave Markee on bass completed the line-up of this studio band. Dave Markee was tall and cheerful, a bit of a raver in those days, though he had come into the rock business from music college (Trinity) on double bass, via £5-per-night jazz sessions at the Bull's Head in Barnes with the Phil Seaman Quartet. This had led to session work and bass guitar, culminating in Georgie Fame's band, which is how he had first recorded with Glyn.

'He called me up and said, "I've got this session with this young girl who doesn't really know what she's doing." That was his mandate – "We really need help to put this thing together. Would you like to come and put in a couple of sessions?" Glyn would never fully book you for an album until he was sure. He'd just take a session and test the water out.'

Olympic Studios in Church Road, Barnes, south of the Thames, was Glyn's 'home territory' at this time. It was a large place, and well suited to his 'live' sound method. There was a small booth where Joan could play her acoustic guitar, and the control room was up some stairs so it overlooked the whole studio.

According to Dave Markee: 'Glyn's way of working was to set the artist in the middle of the studio and get the musicians round then he'd sit with us and say, "Right, play the song." So Joan would play the song – she looked very shy. I guess she must have been nervous, but she covered it very well. I can't remember what the first song was, but I know it was in pieces.'

'The songs were not all very straightforward,' Dave Mattacks confirms, 'and I recall her being very reluctant to sing along, and us just counting bars. They didn't have conventional structures and when she just plays them through you're not really sure what's the verse, what's the chorus, what's the bridge – they all change in strange places.'

Primed by Glyn, the mood of the musicians was supportive. 'It must have done a lot for her,' says Dave Markee, 'that people with a bit more experience than she were so into her music. For us it was like a breath of fresh air, suddenly finding ourselves in a studio with one of the greatest producers in the world and this young girl who was totally off the wall musically.'

Jerry was also struck by the songs. 'They were great! Very unusual – bit tricky at first. "Down To Zero" was the first track we tackled. We'd sit around the piano and write out a few charts, and between us throw them into some kind of arrangement. I really didn't know how to approach these tunes at all – I didn't know if I should blend styles or whatever, so I just played the first thing that came to mind. Then we were all in the control room listening back, and Joan was very quiet, and everybody seemed happy except her!

'Glyn said, "Now, what do you think, Joan?"

'She didn't really say too much.

'And he said, "Is there something wrong with it?"

'She said, "Yeah."

'"What?" And he finally said, "Is it one of the players not playing the right thing?"

'"Yes."

'"Who?"

'And she said, "Him!" – meaning me! You know! That was an embarrassing moment, because Glyn had actually flown me all the way from Los Angeles to do the thing, and I thought, oh no! But it worked out great in the end – I wasn't playing anything wrong, I just wasn't approaching it the way she expected. She had something in her head. And once she spoke up and we knew what was going on it was fine. Otherwise she wouldn't have asked me to join the band!'

Even Dave Markee says, 'Never heard anything quite like Jerry before. And of course Joan was just the most unusual I'd ever come across. And sparks started to fly then. As we were doing the first couple of playbacks I couldn see Glyn getting quite excited about it. And we ended up cutting the first track that night – there was a real buzz around. I remember thinking, I've never heard anything quite like this. I don't just mean the material, but the combination of Glyn's sound and the musicians that he'd got together – it was just different.'

With the initial awkwardness over, the album proceeded very smoothly. The sessions were evenings, booked from seven to ten and they seldom went on past midnight. Glyn would walk in at five to seven, 'Right – let's go!' Joan would strum through the song until everyone had an idea of how it went, then Glyn would go up to the control room and Joan would go into her soundproof booth with her Ovation guitar.

'She'd go in there and sing it and play it,' remembers Dave Markee. 'We'd stop and start for a couple of hours, and eventually hit on an arrangement. Have a little break and then come back and do it. Glyn would turn all the lights down to create a mood before the tape rolled. He'd always be right there – *"That sounds great!"* You know – *"Oh, that's wonderful!"* And we'd invariably get it in a couple of takes. The beauty of Glyn was, he'd never let you rest, always keep chivvying you along, wanting the best out of you, so of course you rose to the occasion.'

Many of the songs were recorded in three hours. 'There wasn't any time to worry about it – no time to think, oh well, are we going to get this or aren't we? If somebody had a good idea for a song he'd let them go with it. I never ever felt chopped off.'

Glyn believed in getting the sounds right at source, out in the studio, not correcting them afterwards on the desk. He used minimal mikes on drums – just bass drum, maybe snare and a couple of overheads. Dave Mattacks was delighted with the results.

'He is really a great producer. He always gets good sounds – I remember him coming up with some great ideas. I was knocked out when he put that delayed echo on the snare in "Love And Affection" – that just blew me away! And he was doing it manually. I remember I said, "What device is that?" And he said, "I'm just pushing up the echo after you've hit the snare."'

Kenny Jones, The Faces' drummer, played on two tracks, 'Down To Zero' and 'Help Yourself'. He was one of Glyn's circle of musicians. On two tracks – 'Water With The Wine' and 'Join The Boys' – Dave Mattacks and Kenny both played, with Dave Markee trying to hold down the beat!

'It was awkward at times for a bass player to sit in the middle of those two. I had to try and state things very strongly, carving a path down the middle. Their feels were entirely different. Ken was always on the back of the beat and Dave would be into his party pieces. There was a lot of kidding going on, good natured showing off. They obviously admired each other a lot.'

The bass would be DI-ed [direct injection – plugged straight into the mixing desk). 'No EQ on it,' (equalizers – tone controls] remembers Dave Markee, 'in fact Glyn and I used to laugh about "Plug it in and play it!" The beauty about it was that he expected you actually to get the sound – his fingers wouldn't go to the desk. "You play it," he used to say, "and I'll record it."

'I've not met anybody since that excited me as a musician and brought out the best in me – and all of us. He was not always an easy guy to work with; in fact at times he was a real pain in the neck – and I guess so were we as well, you know. But it was always *his* session – very old-school – "I'm the boss." '

This combination of enthusiasm and firmness was just what Joan needed. After her run-in with Pete Gage, Joan had changed her attitude, but if she still had any qualms about going into the studio, Glyn had found the secret. As Joan says, 'Well, it's just got to be confidence, really. When we did the album he kept saying, "You can really play that guitar." And I believe him. So I thought, "Oh, all right then – I'll do this album for Glyn." Not just for him, but I made a special effort to try to do it really well – because he seemed to believe that I could do it. I played the guitar better than on any other album, and better than I've ever played onstage, and that was purely because of Glyn saying, "You're good, Joan – get on and do it." '

She also approved of his hands-off approach – keeping to the control room and only offering advice if it was sought. 'If something wasn't happening he'd come and sort things out, very simply – or not so simply!' And she chuckled.

Joan was certainly different this time. Everyone noticed how shy she was, but no one described her as moody. 'I wouldn't say she was completely relaxed, any more than she was tense,' Dave Mattacks feels. 'She'd obviously been in a studio before, working with musicians. A little private, but she seemed fine.'

As Jerry puts it, 'Oh, she was great! She was very shy and introverted – and so was I. But after that first embarrassing moment everything seemed to go smoothly.'

Knowing Glyn, Dave Markee sensed Joan's response. 'I think she knew right from the off that there was not going to be any messing about – not on this one. Glyn would never suffer fools gladly. You wanted to be a prat, mate – out the door! Either that or he'd leave. If the musicians ever got into any ego trips he'd be out – he'd call the session and go home. "That's it!"'

'So it was obvious that he wasn't going to take any nonsense, but he was *so encouraging* with her. And he did it in an incredible way – he would let her hear how good she was, and let it speak for itself. I think in a sense she was very raw, and Glyn tended to strip that right down to basics, really, so it was like her raw talent that was coming out. A remarkable man – he had a real grasp of the psychology needed, and he had a great love for music and creativity. He loved it so much that he would not compromise it, and he would not allow his musicians or his artists ever to compromise it either. And I respect and admire him for that. Wonderful – the heart of the man.

'I think we knew at least half-way through the album that we were onto something quite remarkable. He handled her very, very well, and ended up getting some vocals out of her which were ... lovely, I think, gorgeous. That was about the size of that first one.'

Pete Gage casts a slightly different light on the session.

'When Joan was about three or four weeks into that album I got a call, she was in Olympic and could I come over? So I said, "Well, why?"'

'And she said, "Well, I'd like you to come down to the studio and take a listen to what we're doing." And she sounded a little bit down.

'I said, "Why – is there a problem?"'

'She said, "I'm doing my vocals – it's Glyn, I don't really know what he's doing and I'm a bit worried, and I'd like you to come down and tell me what you think."'

'I said, "Joan, I can't do that – I'm not walking in. . . . If Glyn invited me down that would be something else. I'm quite happy to have a word with Glyn and if he wants to invite me by, that's fine, but I can't just turn up at your session."'

'Well, I spoke to Glyn and he said, "Oh yeah, come on by, I'd love to see you."'

'I think I went down the following night. And I saw exactly what the problem was, because Glyn is well known as being very hard-faced and very, very blunt with people that he works with. And he was literally just telling Joan to go out in the studio, sing your song, taking the faders down [volume controls], sitting by the console, just chatting with his mates. At the end of the track he'd go, "Right, what d'you think of that, darling?"

'To which she'd say, "Well, I don't know."

' "Well, you're the star, aren't you? You know whether it's good or bad or indifferent. Do you want to do it again? Or is that the take?" So she was getting actually no feedback.

'As it so happens, obviously it was working. He'd never have got away with that if he'd had the first Joan Armatrading. Never ever. And of course she knew how the songs went because she had worked them out with The Movies.'

Dave Mattacks says, 'Joan was fairly sure about the general structure. The stuff on the *Love And Affection* album was a combination of her format and structure and with some ideas of Glyn's thrown in.'

Jerry Donahue said 'Down To Zero' was in pieces, and remembers that in these early days she didn't seem to have clear ideas about arrangements beyond her own voice and guitar. 'She pretty much deferred to Glyn, at first, and I think she welcomed any ideas that the musicians had. She's grown to be much more in charge since. She knows very much what she wants these days – and she probably did then. I think she had difficulty expressing herself musically – so she allowed the producer that sort of control.'

But this certainly didn't mean she took a back seat. Jerry, for all his experience and expertise, ended up doubling a lot of what she was playing. 'That was all her doing – she came up with some great riffs. I still haven't heard anyone play the guitar quite like she plays – that acoustic – with such attack. It's great!'

'Of course,' says Dave Markee, 'for my money the best track on the album obviously was "Love And Affection". But I think it was in three or four bits when she brought it in. It started with, "I'm doing this, and then I'm doing that, and then I want to do this ..." sort of thing. And then she'd play it and you'd go, "What? This is never gonna hang together in a week." And you'd go, "Well, Joan, if you do that there ... I don't know how to get from this to that." I'd scratch my head and say, "Well, hang on, love, let's just – what's this?" and try to get inside of it. We'd eventually come out with something that gelled.'

'It's a funny song,' says Joan – 'it's actually a couple of songs in one, but I managed to get them to work, so obviously it doesn't sound like it wasn't just one complete thing.'

'I came up with this bass line that seemed to please everybody,' says Dave, 'and Glyn ended up arranging the whole thing around it. I was always hearing bass lines as soon as she started to play, and they all fitted. I never found it difficult with Joan.

'Joan seemed a bit blown away, by the way it all happened – this combination of Glyn and the musicians getting together these scraps and bits that she'd bring along. But when that remarkable sound came together I can remember her smiling. I know she was very nervous about putting vocals on. Nobody was around when that happened. . . .

'Glyn ended up saying, "Oh, it's not a guitar solo – it's got to be sax solo." '

Jimmy Jewell was the sax player, a down-to-earth character who likes a pint. 'It was a Glyn Johns special – "Can you get down here in an hour?" or something. The recording itself – I probably wasn't there more than half an hour at the most.'

Joan and Glyn Johns were there alone with the tape operator. Glyn played him the track. There were no strings yet, but there were some deep backing vocals.

'Well, I wasn't there when they recorded the rhythm section, but Glyn was doing his usual, "I'm in charge" bit, so I assumed there were lots of things that had been suggested but had been arranged by Glyn. Cos it is a very nice track that – everything came together really well. Glyn's really good at that – I mean, I've fallen out with him in the past – we've nearly come to blows at various points! But he is very good at what he does, albeit a pain in the ass sometimes. In fact, he's a funny guy – he's not given credit for a lot of things that he has done. It seems that anybody who makes it dumps him as a producer and goes on to somebody else.'

The immortal solo was soon achieved.

'Glyn just said, "Listen to this and blow." And I think I just did two takes, and he said, "Great!"'

'I went, "Nooo!"'

'But he said, "I'm the boss – go down the pub."'

'So I said, "Forget it." I took the eighteen quid or whatever it was and . . .'

The next time Joan and Jimmy met was at the Hammersmith Odeon.

'Down To Zero' opens with poise and confidence, the proud voice irresistibly catching our attention, telling us about an all-too-familiar experience in completely new words. Joan's poetry here is very sophisticated, using rhyme and metre casually, contrasting clipped phrases – 'Oh the feeling/ when you're reeling' with conversational ones – 'You step lightly thinking you're number one' – an impossible vocal line which, in Joan's mouth, dances delicately across the beat. Joan writes purple passages – 'Moored to your heel/ let the waves/ come a rushing in' – and dry observation – 'rushing to the mirror/ brush your eyebrows and say/ there's more beauty in you/ than anyone.' We also encounter for the first time Joan's deliberate gender mixing – 'brand new dandy ... steals your man ... she put trouble in your heart ... your Mother's only son ...' This is not casual, Joan is deliberately aiming to speak to everyone. Her study of emotion is very personal but not in the least self-indulgent.

The music is liquid gold, instruments blending perfectly, a burnished sound which denies the fact that they are electric and acoustic, plucked, strummed and struck. The sound has the unity of a string quartet and forms the perfect setting for a smooth, mellow voice, lips to microphone to catch every nuance. The only rawness now is in the emotions, and the music is so seductive that it could flow over us unjudged. There is also greater consistency in sound between the different tracks. No wonder Glyn Johns rated this his best album yet – it is a producer's triumph.

Is it Joan's triumph too? Well for many this will always be the classic album – Joan's finest hour. Of course that is a matter of taste, and there is no reason why it shouldn't be. Since then Joan has been through many musical changes while following her own intentions.

There are classics here: 'Down To Zero' and 'Love And Affection'. But lesser songs like 'Join The Boys' and 'People' have us returning to the mood of a funky band doing its thing which we heard on *Back To The Night*, and to less effect. Perhaps she wrote them with a live set in mind.

On this album Joan clearly establishes the themes and roles which will concern her throughout her work. She displays strength and weakness – the negative paranoia of 'People', strength with vulnerability in 'Down To Zero'; the need for love but lack of trust in

'Somebody Who Loves You' and the sense of being in someone's power: 'Like Fire' and 'Save Me'; Pam's disapproving friend saying 'Help Yourself', and dismissing the stereotypical male who is 'Tall In The Saddle' (inspired by seeing how short John Wayne was when he got off his horse!).

One mood we never quite see again, perhaps because she captured it so definitively, is the elegant seduction of 'Love And Affection'. The invitation is so direct, yet entirely subtle. She manages to convey invitation and passion without vulgarity. This is consummate poetry – like Shakespeare it speaks to everyone. 'I am not in love/ but I'm open to persuasion' – no songwriter has spoken to us like this before. Sometimes the words tumble out with a fine disdain for bar-line or metre: 'Sing me another love song/ but this time/ with a little dedication/ sing it sing it.' Joan's ear for gospel gives them a rhythmic urgency which catches the blood-rushing excitement of the moment. And the sound portrays the shifting meaning – seductive, mysterious, sending shivers down the spine. The soaring sax solo is a climax, but the song winds down again to end in a fluttering scale.

'It *is* a good song,' Joan affirms. 'It's a bloody good song. I wanted it to be the single from the album but A&M weren't too keen. So I fought for it and eventually they released it and it became a hit.

'I'm really pleased with this album. Although, having said that, there's nothing you do that comes out the way you want it – not one hundred per cent. Why? Because I can't explain properly and exactly to either the producer or the musicians what I want.

'If I can talk to one person who gets used to the way I talk then puts it across to the rest, that's fine. Usually it's the producer. But I resent it because I see him putting his own bits in. I know I shouldn't mind. If it was left to me I'd just confuse everybody.'

But Joan has no wish to deny Glyn's essential part. 'I made the album for Glyn. You'd do anything for someone with that much faith in you.'

SEVEN

Oh the feeling

Presumably Derek Green was relieved when he heard the tape of the album. At all events, when *Joan Armatrading* was released in August 1976, A&M swung in hard behind it with almost unprecedented publicity. They took full-page ads in the music and national press and frequent slots on Capital Radio. As Pam Nestor puts it, 'The only reason I listened to the *Love And Affection* album was because it was saturation – I couldn't move without hearing it.'

Once again A&M were writing their own reviews and the campaign took rather a pretentious tone, but then Joan's music seemed to live up to everything that was claimed for it.

'*Joan Armatrading* is one of the most original albums of '76. But will you listen?' etc. 'Forget the hard, hard sell . . . Just listen to the album.'

This time people did listen, and recognition brought an unprecedented spate of interviews. *Sounds* and *Melody Maker* gave her one and two pages. Phil Sutcliffe drew a list of likes from Joan: Spike Milligan, bitter lemon, Gary Glitter, *The Beano*, Van Morisson, drawing cartoons, Sparky, The Who, the silhouette picture of herself on *Back To The Night* (but *not* the aggressive shot on the back of *Joan Armatrading*), John Martyn, *The Little Prince* by Antoine de Saint-Exupéry, driving her new DAF, and *The Black Mikado* – she had seen it three times. She also liked her own name – 'one of the best things about my father. I get into trouble with it sometimes though. I booked the

66

Wigmore Hall for rehearsals once and when I gave my name at the desk the woman said, "We don't allow carpenters here." '

In *Melody Maker* under the heading, 'Joan – burning like fire', Richard Williams gave the album a warm and detailed review, saying not only that it was the most fascinating album he had heard this year, but that the only solo performers who might better it would be Paul Simon or Joni Mitchell.

Back to back with this review on a two-page spread was Caroline Coon's interview. She went to meet Joan at a rehearsal with her new tour band at the small but friendly PSL studio in south London. Jerry Donahue and Dave Mattacks from the album sessions had been joined by Pat Donaldson on bass, also ex-Fairport Convention, but at this time fresh from Chris Spedding's band. (Dave Markee, to his everlasting regret, had allowed Glyn Johns to persuade him into another project, so he never played live with Joan, although he did work with her again on the next two albums.)

It was a warm afternoon and Joan was simply dressed in sand-coloured shirt over blue jeans and bare feet in sandals: '... beneath her plain clothes she suggests a unisex eroticism.' She was relaxed but intent, and the studio atmosphere was charged with respect. After the rehearsal Joan went back to Caroline Coon's place for coffee. 'She sat in an armchair, crossed her legs and pulled a soft hat well down over her eyes. "I like this hat," she says. "It's good for hiding under." '

But Joan was about to come out from hiding – just a little. Talking about her early life in St Kitts and then in Birmingham, she said, 'We were very poor. And they still are. I had a letter from my mum a couple of days back asking for some money to get them food.'

As Caroline praised the album Joan countered with, 'I don't believe anybody when they tell me I'm good,' but went on to confess that she was really pleased with it. Asked how personal her songs are, she claimed, 'They are never about me. Always about someone else.'

Surely she draws on her own experiences?

'No, not really. I can honestly say "no". What I'm saying is that, really, I haven't had that many relationships you see. My relationships are usually ... but we won't go into that.'

'Isn't it impossible to write songs without them having just a little something to do with the person who writes them?'

'All right, they've got something to do with me. But they're not

67

drawn from my experiences. You might get one or two that are directly to do with me. But it's mostly other people.'

Caroline mentions the song 'People'.

'Oh "People". All right, that's to do with me. That's obviously to do with me. And yes, all right, "Steppin' Out" too. All right, all right, there's always one!'

On 'Save Me' – 'I've no idea what that song's about,' she insisted.

But after claiming to have made up 'Water With The Wine' she relents and tells the story.

'I was going home to Hayes one night, and there was this boy. He was only young, eighteen or whatever. I was waiting for the train and he was doing circles around me. When I get into the train I was the only one in the compartment. And up comes this little lad, takes off his hat saying, "Can I sit by you please." I said, "All right then," and we chat.

'Then I get off at my stop and he says, "I get off here too. I work around the corner. Can I walk you to your door?" Well, he does, and he obviously doesn't want to go, so I ask him in for a cup of coffee. I play a record and give him an apple or something, and I ask him to go off to work, and that was it. That's all that happened. But the song was about what I knew was in his mind. His name was Donald.'

By now the verbal fencing between Joan and Caroline was good-humoured. Perhaps Joan relates better to women than to men?

'My best friends are women, yes. But how can I answer that question? It depends on the situation. If it's business then I'm only dealing with men. But in a social situation I'm only dealing with women ... I don't know many blokes, actually, to tell the truth. Obviously I know the guys I work with, but I don't socialize with them. It's just me. All the people who have visited me since I moved into my new flat have been women.'

Does she love women more than men?

'Yes, well, they're prettier, aren't they? But that's got nothing to do with it. Whether you're in love with a woman or a man, all you're talking about is people. If you're talking about how often you've been in love, it has nothing to do with a man or a woman, all it has to do with is how often.

'I don't know what will happen in a couple of years, but I've never felt the need to live with anyone. I've seen so many people break up, and it's "I bought the curtains", "I bought the sofa", and all that. Which is pointless. I can't be bothered with someone walking out with half the furniture when they go. Living with someone, you lose a lot of freedom and independence, and I don't want to lose that yet.

'Being in love used to be quite important to me. There was a time when I thought it would be nice to have somebody around, somebody to chat to and go out with. But really it's not that important any more. Probably because I've seen so many people, one day in love and the next it's all over.

'If I'm in love, I don't know whether I'm any happier. But I'm a lot calmer. It doesn't always make it easier to work, though, because you can sort of sit back then, can't you? Take after the time I recorded *Back To The Night*. I wasn't with anybody then. It was a turning point in my life, though, and I was happier about everything. I wrote loads of songs. I'm happiest when I spend all my time trying to achieve what I want in my music.'

This interview is the frankest Joan has ever given, admitting that many of her songs do derive – however obliquely – from personal feelings and experiences. She has made some neat points against this conclusion – that you don't have to commit a murder to write about murder, and that if she had been through all the experiences the songs cover, her life would have been so crowded and turbulent she'd have had no time for writing. But this is to assume that every song must refer to a different event, whereas a single emotional experience may give rise to several very different songs as it is re-examined in the creative or subconscious mind. Equally several situations and characters may come together to suggest a single song, and these need not be Joan's own experiences. Like parables, Joan uses them to make her own emotional point, and this is where she becomes personal. There are themes and situations which Joan keeps re-examining. Nevertheless, the inevitable conclusion – despite Joan's constant denials – is that some songs do refer to experiences which have touched her deeply.

Rehearsals and interviews over for now, Joan and the band took off for the States before 'Love And Affection' was released and before the album had begun to nudge its way into the charts. 'It was pretty much a club tour,' says Jerry Donahue. 'I can remember opening for Richie Havens at the Bottom Line in New York, and playing a lot of clubs – the Main Point in Pennsylvania, outside of Philadelphia.'

The band was in excellent shape and they had a good sound man, so sound checks became a chance to relax and enjoy an occasional jam session. Dave Mattacks recalls, 'Joan used to like to play slow 6/8 or 12/8 blues, and she'd pick up Jerry's guitar and have a go. When we rehearsed, I remember her saying, "There's some older numbers I'd like you to learn from albums way back." And she must have been introducing new ones as they were coming up. I know that we were playing "Show Some Emotion" live.'

Joan was now becoming a more experienced performer. She certainly seemed more relaxed before going on stage. 'If she was tense, she didn't show it,' says Jerry. 'She seemed very cool. Always in control.'

Towards the end of the tour guitarist Albert Lee joined the band. As the result of a booking error, Jerry had to miss the last two gigs. 'So Albert joined and we played together for the last part of the tour, then he did it on his own for those last two dates. Joan really liked the sound of the two of us playing together, so she asked Albert to play on the British tour too – also because he played very good piano as well. It was during that time we did that *Live At The Bijou Café* album in Philadelphia.'

A&M, keen to break Joan in the States, hit on the idea of a live promotional album to send to disc jockeys. This rare recording has tremendous energy and excellent playing from the whole band. The first track, 'Join The Boys', has a 2/4 feel as band opinion seems divided as to which is the first beat of the bar, but Dave Mattacks nimbly solves the problem. Pat Donaldson is a busier bass player than Dave Markee. Albert Lee's guitar is superb, though he draws our attention more than anything in Glyn Johns's productions. Performances are sensitive, but Joan sings out more than in the intimacy of the studio.

'Cool Blue' is more relaxed and atmospheric than in the studio – the hot sun and cool drink. 'Dry Land' she plays solo, at the piano, with a lighter voice, but more urgency than on *Back To The Night*. (Pam, who wrote the words, says Joan played 'Dry Land' with tremendous feeling live, which was not captured on the studio album.) This is followed by a lively solo version of 'Steppin' Out' to the delight of the vocal American crowd. 'Love And Affection' is more soulful and gospelly, drawing an excited response during the number. A lively

'Water With The Wine' and moody 'Tall In The Saddle' round off an excellent collection.

After the show in Nashville Joan had a less friendly encounter with members of the audience.

'I met four black guys. They got really angry that I had a whole load of white musicians. They said they really liked the way I played and sang, but they reckoned if I sang proper black lyrics – whatever they are – I'd be better.'

Dave Mattacks remembers the incident. 'I was hanging about having a drink, and from what I can recall she was being harassed a *little* bit by some black guys. The gist of it was, "How come you're using white musicians?" And I heard her strong reply to the effect – she didn't use these words – but basically, "Don't give me any of that crap – if I can find black musicians that play the way these guys play, then I'll use them. At the moment I'm quite happy with these and they're fine." And I remember the guy was kind of pinned by the wall, eyes open, and she was wagging the finger at him, giving him all that!'

'I was aware of black culture problems in America,' Joan says, 'but I don't dwell on them. If something affected me strongly enough, I'd write about it. I don't really see myself as black or white so much as British.'

Meanwhile back in Britain the album had entered the charts and was getting phenomenal radio play. A British tour was booked for December but it was decided to fly Joan and the band back for a special gig at the Hammersmith Odeon on 23 September – Joan's first big headlining date. When she heard about it she was worried. 'I just hope it's a good idea – I'm not convinced. A tour would be impossible. *All* the people in Britain don't know who I am. In the past I've always supported. I've never had to worry about people coming on the strength of my name.'

She needn't have worried. The Odeon sold out two weeks beforehand. Dave Mattacks was very excited. 'That was the first time I'd ever played the Hammersmith Odeon, I couldn't believe it, I really enjoyed that – the place being full and Joan just went down an absolute storm.'

Jimmy Jewell, who played the sax solo on 'Love And Affection', was booked to come and do the same on stage. After the sound check, 'I went round the pub as usual, and I think Joan must have gone round as well – A&M were in there buying drinks, so *wheee* . . . !

'At that time the backstage officials at Hammersmith were a real pain. They always give you this artist pass thing, but I never used to carry it on principle – I used to throw it away! I've done Hammersmith various times with other people and they knew me, sort of. But I don't think they'd actually given Joan a pass, being that she was the star and all that, and I got back there and she was arguing with them! Instead of telling them to fuck off, she's going, "Oh! Well ...! Picking on me and all...!"'

'I said, "What's the matter, Joan?"'

'"They won't let me in!"'

'And I said, "It's her show, right? If you're not gonna let her in there's no show so I'm going back to the pub!"'

'So they go, "Oh, it's him!" They recognized me – the troublemaker!'

'Then A&M appeared – "Don't you realize who she is?"! – and all this, so everybody got in. But before that it was just paranoia – she got upset and said, "Nobody picks on anybody except me!"'

But Jimmy had his own identity problems later.

'What happened is, I was only doing the one song anyway, right? So I came on and did the song, then my instructions were, stand there, don't go off, cos she's gonna announce you. So I stood there ... and stood there ... and she's looking sort of all... So I went *Grrr!* and walked off, really annoyed. I went upstairs and got changed.

'Then somebody from A&M came in and said, "She forgot your name – sorry!" And I said, "Fucking wonderful! I would have just walked off – I felt like a lemon standing there."

'So he said, "She wants you to come on for the encore!"

'So I said, "I've just got changed – nobody mentioned this earlier." A&M were always a pain in the ass. Anyway, I said, "I'm not getting changed back again – I'll go on as I am." I had white suit and a hat and all that. So I went on and did the encore – we did "Love And Affection" again. I think she actually introduced me this time – somebody had written it down.'

As far as he could remember even Joan wore something different for this gig. 'I think she got changed into something.... Nothing sort of ... Shirley Bassey!'

But from the front everyone was delighted with the gig. All the music papers ran reviews. For *New Musical Express*, David Hepworth reported, 'Audience and performer were galvanized into one of those rare expressions of unity and common purpose in which the noises are less important than the gestures and the simple thrill of being there.' This audience consisted of 'very liberated lesbian couples, serious-looking men in their thirties and collars and ties, soul men, rock-'n'-rollers, a smattering of pseuds and more women than I've ever seen at a comparable gig anywhere ... all seemingly drawn less by her considerable musical talents than by an electric sympathy with what she's singing about.... On "Love And Affection" everyone was with her from the first line.'

Joan says, 'I was nervous throughout the whole show.'

Before returning to the States Joan recorded *The Old Grey Whistle Test* at the BBC theatre on Shepherd's Bush Green, performing 'Down To Zero' and 'Love And Affection' with the band. She also appeared on *Top of the Pops*, this time without the band, but with Jimmy Jewell for the sax solo. The producer had told the other musicians they wouldn't be needed. On this occasion at the Shepherd's Bush television centre there was another unfortunate encounter for Joan.

There is a studio bar, but artists appearing on any show have to get a member of the programme staff to sign them in. Jimmy had been there before and knew the procedure, so he said to Joan, 'Fancy coming for a drink up to the bar?

'And she said, "I've just been up there and they wouldn't let me in!" And I can imagine her doing this freaking out bit. She had this paranoia thing, It-only-happens-to-her. But it doesn't – it happens to everybody, but you've got to handle it in a certain way.'

The backing track had been pre-recorded by the band plus Jimmy, and the others were rather miffed when they were not required for the actual show.

'They had me flying through the air!' Jimmy explains. 'It's very strange. She was singing and then the sax bit came on and I was floating across the screen.'

So Joan and the band returned to tour the States supporting Stephen Stills while the album and single peaked at number twelve and number ten respectively. Decca obtained the distribution rights on the first album and re-released it, with 'Alice' as a single, though neither record sold enough to touch the charts.

On 4 December Joan was back for the *Michael Parkinson Show*, then the British tour kicked off in Edinburgh. By now Joan was receiving the same rapturous response from packed houses that she had at Hammersmith three months before. Needless to say the blend of Joan with these superb session players (including Albert Lee) warmed even the hardest-bitten reviewers, but among the most moving moments were when Joan, the nervousness of Ronnie Scott's far behind her, stepped forward alone to play 'Dry Land' and 'Steppin' Out'. The greatest adoration of course was for 'Love And Affection' – and this was even repeated as the second encore after 'Back To The Night'.

The Christmas issue of *Sounds* carried a front-cover picture – *Joan Armatrading* was voted the best album of the year. Number two was Joni Mitchell with *Hejira*, Steely Dan at number three with *Royal Scam*, and Bob Dylan's *Desire* at number four. Singer, songwriter, Joan, twenty-six years old, had suddenly arrived.

EIGHT

Light up if you're feeling happy

One of the first things Joan bought was a car – a small yellow DAF. She used to drive around wildly, and one night on her way to a fish and chip shop with a friend, she skidded around a corner and terrified a man who was crossing the road. He followed them into the chip shop and shouted and raved while Joan calmly ordered. Finally the man behind the counter said, 'Is this man bothering you, miss?'

'Which man?' returned Joan, deadpan.

Now that everyone was seeking interviews, Joan turned this blank approach to her advantage. In January 1977 *New Musical Express* ran the front-page headline JOAN ARMATRADING – THE WIERDEST INTERVIEW SHE'S EVER DONE. The irrepressible Nick Kent had crossed swords with Ms A and that headline was her own opinion. She started by admitting – or claiming – 'I've actually got very little to say for myself,' nodding and shrugging through the next two questions. She then gave her 'objective approach' account of songwriting. Nick asked her about the last two albums and she explained the detached state she had been in when recording *Back To The Night* and how much happier she felt when working with Glyn Johns. Then he asked her, 'What do you mostly recall about your childhood? Were there any characteristics that stood out? Periods of depression, say? Any grand reminiscences?'

'No. Nothing outstanding.'

'What about boyfriends?'

'I've never had a boyfriend.'

'I'm not trying to pry about . . . uh, your sex-life or anything. I mean a boyfriend like . . . someone you walk hand-in-hand with through a park.'

'Well I've held hands and walked through parks.' And she shrugged.

'Have you ever been in love?'

(Aggressive, taken aback): 'Why do you want to know?'

'Because I'm interested. Anyway you write good love songs.'

'I don't know. I may have been. Couldn't say, really. I mean, sometimes you feel like you are but I . . . I dunno.'

A little talk of comics and the interview was soon over. As Joan finally said, 'You kept asking about me – pointing your questions at me personally. If you'd kept on the subject of music it would have been better.'

Nick Kent realized he was short on copy and went in search of the more talkative Pam Nestor. This interview went better. 'I liked him,' Pam says. 'He was all right. But it was really strange, because when he rang me up he made out he was going to do something on me. And basically what he was doing was, he was writing something on Joan and he just wanted more information.'

For the first time the public heard about *Hair* and how the two women met. Pam also mentioned the manuscript of a book she had written about their time together. 'People who've read it claim that Joan comes out of it as a very, very strong person.'

'Has Joan been in love?' Nick asked. 'Has she ever lost the reins emotionally?'

'Oh, yes,' the answer comes back knowingly, resolute that no details be shed. 'Joan's been in love. I've seen it happen to her.'

For Joan, 1977 kicked off with another American tour.

'West Palm Beach, Miami, Florida is the only time I've been to a gig and not played it because it was so horrible. I walked into the bar, but the whole thing was a bar – there was nowhere for any of us. They had juke boxes, television, pool things – and none of it was going to be off when I was on! I didn't really feel I wanted to compete against all these games and things. So I went back to the hotel, didn't do the gig because I was "taken suddenly ill". And that same night there was an incredible storm, and outside my hotel room was a willow tree, and inside was lizards crawling up the wall! And I was thinking, oh God, I don't want to be here! I wish I had a mate just round the corner or something. So that's where "Willow" came from.'

West Palm Beach excepted, touring was now an enjoyable outing. 'I remember one thing we did,' says Dave Mattacks. 'It must have been indicative of what a good time everyone was having, because we went to the Ovation factory and Donaldson, Donahue and myself all chipped in and bought her a twelve-string. We got a great deal on it and we surprised her with it. That was nice. Everyone was obviously getting on quite well at the time. I think we might have lasted a little bit longer than some of the line-ups. As you probably know, she's got a thing about changing – she doesn't like to use the same musicians all the time.'

When they returned to London to start the next album Dave found himself dropped, though not by Joan. 'I think it was mainly my own fault. I'd been playing some of the new songs live ["Show Some Emotion" etc.], and when we went into the studio Glyn was making suggestions, and in those days I was a little bit stroppy. I said something along the lines of, "Well, I really don't want to play it that way because I don't hear it that way – I'm in charge...." And we fell out for quite a few years, Glyn and I. Understandably – you know. And then Joan just said, "It's time for a change."'

Dave Markee, who had missed the tour, was back playing bass for half the tracks. He feels, 'Glyn was convinced that he always had to move forward. He wanted to use other people to try and get a different spark going, and I suppose that's why he used [Dave] Kemper and [Bryan] Garafolo [Americans – drums and bass]. Also he worked in America and England and he'd want to have different feel – you know, there's a way that English people play rock-'n'-roll, and a way Americans do, and he wanted different styles.'

So for the 'British' tracks Glyn called up Henry Spinetti, who had played drums for Joan in 1972, though Glyn didn't know this. 'It was great to walk in and go, "Nice to see you – lovely!" And for me it was some of the best recording sessions I'd ever done with Glyn. I thought he was wonderful, especially for a drummer, because of the old miking technique. And he was good on tempos – he was right there with you, nodding along there.'

Joan liked Henry's whacky sense of humour. She is not renowned for making jokes, but friends say Joan has a good, dry wit, and she always enjoyed a laugh. These sessions were also more relaxed as they were back at Olympic with a successful album behind them.

This time they started at 2 p.m. Once again Glyn and the musicians would gather round while Joan played them the song. They still had to coax her to sing, and then she would mumble a bit and they would coax her some more. Joan was more confident this time, though still shy, and she either had a clearer idea of what she wanted, or else was more prepared to express it. She wasn't always asking, 'What do you think?' And yet the musicians felt they could be freer with suggestions. The whole process was more open, though just as meticulous.

Usually the shape of an arrangement would be thrashed out by four, then Glyn would go to the control room, Joan would shut herself in her booth and they would start running the song down for sound, the musicians trying out different ideas. Joan played acoustic guitar, sometimes singing a line to guide the musicians over a tricky change. Joan always sang well, but these vocals couldn't be used as her guitar would be audible on the guide vocal track.

Joan still occasionally had difficulty explaining what she wanted and sometimes it was well into the evening and the song still in pieces. Then Glyn would step in. He had 'huge amounts' of patience, as Henry puts it, but when a song was clearly bogged down he would take charge and tell Henry, 'When I go like *this* – stop!' 'So I'd look up, playing the feel, and he'd go like this and you'd stop. "When I go like *that* – you pick up on the drum fill."' Occasionally the musicians would see Glyn and Joan having 'vigorous discussions' in the sound-proof control room, but differences were always sorted out in the end. Generally it was Glyn, as producer, who had the last word.

On one occasion, though, it was more democratic. As Joan puts it, 'On "Opportunity" I really didn't want to play that guitar solo, but everyone else refused to.'

Finally Dave Markee says of Joan, 'She was always pleasant to work with, but I think – what can I say? – she always struck me as somebody who would not give her heart easily. That's about the nub of it. So there was a holding back emotionally from her, though in the studio context that doesn't really matter.'

On the final record there was no holding back of emotions. The opening track is one of the most startling, riveting openers on any album ever, an achingly vivid study in paranoia. Glyn Johns captures the atmosphere of tension as Joan tugs on the strings of her perfectly recorded guitar and whines like an old blues singer. The mood is heightened by the timid sound of thumb-piano.

'The African thumb-piano,' Joan remembers – 'I just picked that up too. I saw Taj Mahal use it in one of his shows and he really made it sing. I forgot about it for years, then when I'd finished "Woncha Come On Home" I thought, "Yeah!" and I nipped out and got it, put it on and it sounded great. I tune it myself – I've no idea what the traditional tunings are.'

Show Some Emotion is an even more intimate album than *Joan Armatrading*. It has fewer stories and is more like a succession of love letters. 'Show Some Emotion' itself is a wonderfully direct song, recalling Pam Nestor's complaint about the closed, secretive personality of the English. Joan says, '"Show Some Emotion" was written after watching a group of men talking. One was laughing, but had no expression. His eyes just weren't reflecting what his face was doing.'

'Warm Love' might be a reply to 'Show Some Emotion', someone in love despite herself – or possibly himself: 'Let me be ... your one Romeo'. Joan is concerned with weakness and strength throughout her writing, and this is one of Joan's 'victim' songs. There are several songs here where she is in over her head in some way or other – 'Woncha Come On Home', 'Opportunity', 'Mama Mercy'. But she seldom gives way to her own weakness – either she is railing against it or else we feel it is her inner strength which gives her the courage to parade or examine her weakness. This is an important part of Joan's appeal, especially set against the uncanny truthfulness of so many of her lyrics. Time and again she strikes a chord as we recognize a closely observed emotion, perhaps something which we had never identified quite so clearly in ourselves.

All of which makes 'Never Is Too Late' a curious anomaly. 'The reason I wrote that was, I was walking along the pavement in New York one day and a guy broke a bottle on the side of a wall and he started hacking away at his wrist. I rushed into this shop to phone an ambulance, and someone else did it before me, and the ambulance came and took him away.

'There's so many crazy people there. I was walking along the street again and this woman comes down the road, and all of the inside of her mouth was hanging out – it was really bloated, red, bulbous, and it made me feel really bad. And I wanted to go up to her and say, "Do you want some money for the operation . . . ?" I started to cry, of course. And I stopped and turned round and watched her go – I was thinking, blimey, I'm too late. And that's really why I wrote that song. Cos I wasn't too late. I could've run after her and given her the money. It's like saying, "It's *not* too late" and "Never doing it *is* too late".' But the song is about wanting the courage to approach someone in a bar – rather like thinking of some real-life torture to make the dentist's chair easier to handle!

Musically Joan explores the different styles she has always drawn upon, but the diversity is held together by Glyn's steady hand. Gospel is more evident on this album. On 'Peace In Mind' it is emphasized by Joan's piano – rare since the first album. 'Mama Mercy', a study of panic in words and music, could be straight out of *The Blues Brothers*.

The most popular song on *Show Some Emotion* is 'Willow'. Conventionally men are supposed to protect women, but it was not a man who wrote 'Willow'. As a woman's song, it broadens the normal supportive role to something far stronger. In fact it is a wonderful message to come from either sex, and perhaps all the greater for not offering protection as a kind of cage – there is no hint of possessiveness here.

'Kissin' And A Huggin'' is the first of Joan's 'me and my baby flaunting our love in public' songs. (More pointed is 'Taking My Baby Up Town' on the next album.) In this song there is a subtle shift from the third-person 'Took my babe walking' to 'And you talked of love to me' – another example of the gender blur which may give Joan's songs a more universal appeal.

Show Some Emotion went to number six in the charts, but neither 'Willow' nor the title track scored as singles, despite Ray Coleman's review in *Melody Maker* which concluded: '*Show Some Emotion* seems to me an absolutely essential item for the collection of anyone with the remotest interest in today's music, presenting as it does one of our finest singers delivering a searing collection of songs. There would appear to be about half a dozen potential hit singles on the album too. What an album!'

All summer Joan had been working her way through her fourth

tour of the States, this time with an all-American band – mostly the personnel from the last album. Jerry Donahue was the only familiar face, and he had been joined by Bryan Garafolo and David Kemper on bass and drums, plus Red Young on keyboards and Quitman Dennis on horns. These last two gave the band a fuller sound to keep the live band up to Glyn Johns's studio polish.

America was a tough nut to crack – 'In Philadelphia they may know who you are but ten miles up the road you could be anyone.' Joan was trying to break through in the States the hard way, and her tours became notorious among musicians for the stamina required.

'The band members will tell you I'm a slave-driver – and I am to a degree. It's not just that I like to work, but once I start I really work.'

In October she came back to tour Britain, and Robin Katz of *Record Mirror* caught her in an optimistic and unusually communicative mood.

'This is the strongest band I've worked with yet. David Kemper has made the biggest difference. He's very powerful. When he hits hard you really know it. Am I worried about being overpowered by my own band? No, not at all. It's my material they're playing. If they overpower me it's still my song that comes through.

'Life on the road doesn't allow you much time in one place for anything. Figure – you're up at seven, at the airport at nine and on a plane by ten. By the time you get where you have to go you drop your things at the hotel and rush to the gig for a sound check. From the sound check you might have a chance for a quick bite at the hotel. Then you have the gig and it's back to the hotel.

'I do my best writing after a show. Back at the hotel is the largest pocket of time there is. If I don't write I read.'

Joan confided that she sometimes went a couple of months without putting pen to paper.

'But then I may turn around and do ten songs in two days. The more I write the better chance I have of coming up with something good. I usually start by writing too many words to sing reasonably with one breath. Then I'll slow down and try to sort out the lyrics so I can say the same thing with fewer words. Then I'll leave it for a few days. I'll put the music on. If the music fits the lyrics, that's it, I'm satisfied and I'll leave the song.'

Dublin was the first gig of the tour and it showed Joan had taken a big step forward in ability and confidence. The months of touring had honed Joan and her musicians into a fine band. 'Down To Zero' opened the set, sounding much fuller than with any previous line-up. When someone in the crowd shouted, 'You'll never be as big as Maria Callas!' Joan came right back with, 'I don't eat as much!' – a far cry from the nervous performer of previous years. And later when she blew the opening of 'Opportunity' she just stopped and said, 'I really made a fool of myself there – and me a professional!' and went on to deliver a stunning performance of the song. 'Willow', the new single, came early in the set – it had yet to take its place as the big singalong encore.

Joan gave a haunting account of 'Wontcha Come On Home' accompanied by Red Young on finger-piano, then brought up the energy with a solo acoustic 'Steppin' Out'. The set naturally featured numbers from the last two albums, but also included 'Cool Blue', now expanded to a major stage number. 'Tall In The Saddle' ended the set to rapturous applause, then the encore was 'Back To The Night'.

The tour wound its way around the country, finally coming to the Hammersmith Odeon – two nights sold out and an extra one added. One of these shows was filmed by BBC television, but Joan and the band were distracted by the cameras, and the audience by the lights. 'That's probably the worst show I've ever done.' Joan certainly hated seeing the broadcast the following year – 'people will look at this mess and think that's how I really am.' But 'the next night was amazing, a great show', a fitting end to the year in which Joan had had her first gold album – *Joan Armatrading* had sold over 150,000 and spent twenty-five weeks in the American charts. In the British charts it had only reached number twelve, but *Show Some Emotion* went into the top ten at number six, Joan's highest position yet, and later that year it too went gold.

NINE

Keep on pushing

In 1978 it was back into the studio, with Joan still reeling from the tour. This was Joan's third collaboration with Glyn Johns, producing a tighter album than the previous two. Joan was deliberately trying for a different process.

'I wanted it to be more of a rock album – not a rock-'n'-roll album in the Chuck Berry sense but one that has a tougher, less formal feel to it.'

She wanted to combine the energy of a live performance and the quality of studio sound, with hardly any overdubs. To this end she worked with half the number of musicians, a real studio band, but she did not simply take her live band into the studio.

'Sometimes you have a band that gets so used to doing a song one way that its hard for them to go into a studio and change it. That's not a put-down on the musicians, because I've always been very lucky with the people I've worked with, it's just a fact.'

Dave Markee and Henry Spinetti stayed from the last album on bass and drums. From Joan's live band, the American Red Young played piano and Quitman Dennis played a curious electronic wind instrument, the Lyricon. 'I don't think anybody liked it much,' says Dave Markee. 'I think he was experimenting, trying to find his way on it.'

Dick Simms from Eric Clapton's band played organ and accordion and the band was completed by a young guitar player, Phil Palmer.

83

Phil had slipped into session playing almost by chance, being the nephew of Ray and Dave Davies of The Kinks. They used him with various artists on their Konk label and he went on to do an Iggy Pop album with David Bowie, and work with David Essex and Frank Zappa.

'It was quite early on in my career as a session man. I remember arriving at Olympic at ten o'clock on a Monday morning, and being confronted with Glyn Johns, who was then the bee's-knees producer, and then a bit later, Joan. I thought, well, bugger the nerves, I'll go and say Hello and introduce myself. So I went over to her and said, "Hello – I'm Phil Palmer."

'She said, "Oh – you better be good!"

'That was the first thing she ever said to me, and it didn't really put me at my ease, I can tell you. The first three or four days of the project I was just too tense to do anything creative at all. She really put me on edge.'

Olympic was a huge studio and Glyn had the band set up right across it as if they were on stage, with Henry's drums on a rostrum in the middle.

'Glyn always worked like that,' says Henry. 'He used to just record the room. It was the real performance Glyn was looking for. He just took that performance and captured it on tape.'

The spontaneity of the idea worked well for the first week. 'Then,' says Joan, 'it started to get a bit heavy and took forever to get the next lot of songs down. I think we were really excited to start with, you know. Then I began to get very tired – the whole touring thing caught up with me. That's why I don't play any electric guitar on the album.'

This live method had its drawbacks for the musicians. Phil was surprised because, 'There were no screens and everything was leaking onto everything else. Which put the pressure on a bit because in a regular session if you make a mistake you can always go back and fix it. But in this situation if you made a mistake it went on every track.'

Once again Joan played and sang in a separate soundproof booth. 'I think Glyn Johns, being quite an aggressive kind of producer, would force her to go in – I don't think she enjoyed doing it,' says Phil. 'In fact they had quite a few arguments – not audible, but you'd see them in the booth, mouthing....'

Generally though, the sessions went smoothly. Again they started at two. 'It would be a pretty relaxed start,' Henry recalls. 'Some sort of shape would be appearing by about four, and probably work up until about six or seven – trying it, going and listening, have a tea break, crack a joke. Then go and have something to eat, café round the corner or sit there and eat. Then come back and hit it straight off fresh, and it would usually be that one – those couple of takes after getting out of the place. And if it wasn't nowhere at all, well we'd all go home. And then you'd come in for two o'clock start, go for one straight away, and the performance would be there. That was how those sessions were, and I thought they were brilliant.

'I loved working on those old albums with Joan, they were great, particularly with Glyn. Mind you, he was a hard person. But a very soft person – hard exterior, because he had to be, I suppose – especially with some of the musicians, you know. But I think he was quite a softy really. I think they keep in touch now and again [Joan and Glyn]. They ought to, anyway.'

Joan was consciously trying to allow the musicians more space. 'I used to say what to play all the time. Then I was in control, very much so. But I decided I should get out of that way of working because it sometimes made things go stiff, made the musicians feel stale. So now – well, how I play obviously suggests how the songs should sound. Then the musicians play what they think will fit in, so it's slightly improvised. Then if I don't like it we try something else. It is involved because the structures are complicated, but the musicians like to work that way. It's different for them, I think.'

On this album Joan first flirted with reggae. 'My little brother had got hold of some really authentic, raw records, very basic reggae. I've never heard anything like them before. It seemed to me that's the way it should sound, and I tried to get as near to it as I could. We actually did the track 'Bottom To The Top' in one take, and Henry's really excellent on it, he's all over the shop! I mean, he didn't know what was happening. He didn't know where the song began or ended, literally. Apart from me, nobody knew what was happening.'

Even Glyn Johns couldn't help him here. ' "OK, this is reggae, Henry, and it's totally up to you, mate – I don't know much about it," ' Henry recalls. 'And Joan says, "Where I was born the way they play reggae – *do, do-doo, do-doo – boom: do, do-doo, do-doo – boom*. Good luck!" '

'It was funny,' says bass player Dave, 'because Henry, he's Welsh, see, a boyo from the valleys, trying to play reggae. Joan was probably more into that than any of us and I remember feeling very uncomfortable about it. Trying to get Henry to play reggae – it was ... most bizarre.'

Part of Henry's problem was that he went out for a smoke just before the take. (He has given up since leaving the pressure of London. 'I hated to be in that position – can't do anything without rolling up.')

'He came back,' Phil remembers, 'and he's a bit giggly. Glyn said, "OK, let's go then!" and Henry had completely forgotten what the tempo was, everything. Glyn's getting very uptight – "Count in, Henry!" And so Henry just counts in completely blind and we crash through the song ... and *that was the one!* It sounded really good, but the drumming on it is all over the place! But the track sounds great – it's got that loose rawness which is very much part of Joan.'

Everyone who worked with Glyn admired his ability – his magic. But this was the last Armatrading–Johns studio album – to the disappointment of many. As Dave Markee says, 'I don't know why she decided to change producers from Glyn. I could never see the point. Because I don't think she's made such classic records since – it was the combination. Maybe Glyn wanted to move on, maybe she did ... but I always felt sad about that. I'd love to hear her again – with Glyn.'

Neither Dave nor Henry worked with Joan again, though both would have liked to. Looking back on this time, Henry says, 'All I know is, in the beginning we used to laugh a lot. But we all get a bit older.'

To The Limit – perhaps Joan felt she had gone as far as she could with Glyn. She had obviously changed tremendously since first entering a studio, and some of those changes were only now being fully realized. This even shows on the album sleeve – Joan had never shown more than a truncated head or bust but here she is relaxed, open, reclining on her sofa with her comics, looking straight into the lens, challenging. Annie Liebovitz was the first woman to photograph Joan for an album cover. She spent four days in Joan's home, and discovered a new openness, the confidence to be relaxed but determined.

Musically the big change in Joan was from seeing herself as the singer-songwriter, closeted with her acoustic guitar, to becoming a fan of rock music – the heavier the better! With Glyn, Joan had explored the 'Joni Mitchell' side of her writing. The next album would be made in America to a very different beat.

But as with changing musicians, this does not imply dissatisfaction. Joan was very keen on this album – she even had a cassette made of it to play in her car, when normally she never listened to her just-completed work.

'It's still emotional, but less ... emotionally down. "You Rope You Tie Me" could by the lyrics be one depressing number, but how it's sung certainly doesn't sound depressing. The biggest change is in the melodic approach – if I was going to do a melody I wanted to hold it for longer. I'm really chuffed, cos the music turned out just the way I wanted it to.'

To The Limit is an 'aspects of love' album – the songs are like a series of letters or private conversations addressed to the lover.

'Most of the things I see going on around me are unhappy things. It all comes down to love and hate. A lot of people, when they're in love, spend their whole lives fighting to keep it – if they get involved with an affair which is really strong, really passionate. It's as if they're just waiting for it to end. Living with a fear of what might happen in the future before it arrives. They can never be happy with what they have. That's a mistake.'

The first track is confident and up tempo, but a less riveting, moody start than either of the previous albums. 'Barefoot And Pregnant' was a well-known expression in the women's movement, but Joan had only heard it in a chance remark from her agent. 'We were talking about wealth and men with beautiful wives, and how they like to keep that beauty to themselves. They put her in the best house high up on the hill with everything around her and keep her pregnant so she can't go out.' The phrase immediately caught Joan's imagination. 'It sounded so nice – I mean, what it stands for isn't particularly nice at all, but it sounded ... those words together.' The seed of a song.

The quiet piano opening of 'Your Letter' sounds like a return to *Whatever's For Us*, though when the full band comes in there is a broader sweep to the music. 'I was talking to [American singer] Bonnie Raitt, and she mentioned the day before she had found a letter in her bed that she shouldn't have seen ["Between the covers/ And my bare skin"]. Something like that is very strong. I wanted to write about it. On the other hand I didn't want to write about it too obviously like her thing because, well, she was really upset.'

The nasal sound of Quitman Dennis's Lyricon gives an edge to the jaunty, Simon and Garfunkel lilt of Joan's acoustic on 'Am I Blue For You'. A muted electric guitar provides tension in 'You Rope You Tie Me' before the band lets rip in true rock fashion. 'Baby I' completes the first side, Joan's first true love ballad, sentimental and uncomplicated, over simple, gospel chords.

'It was written just as one line after I'd seen the moon looking enormous over Los Angeles, and the rest of the song developed around that.'

The reggae experiment 'Bottom To The Top' ('To The Limit') opens side two, a strange song in which Joan could be talking about a relationship – 'To the limit here we go/ From the bottom to the top'. But it could be Joan urging herself to go for it – 'You know I want first/ And not just a place' – becomes 'I know I want first'.

Then the urgent 'Taking My Baby Up Town' displays even more strongly the theme of 'Kissin' And A Huggin'' – people being outraged by a public show of affection: 'I was walking down the street/ Looking like a million dollars/ With a pretty person on my arm/ When someone started shouting/ They were hooting and a hollering/ They were saying I should never/ Have been born'. Now this describes a situation all too familiar to gay people, as Penny Valentine suggested in her *Melody Maker* interview that September.

'No,' Joan replied firmly. 'It's just about a bloke and his girlfriend.'

Penny pressed the point that this sort of public reaction was surely not a heterosexual problem – 'It hadn't even crossed my mind it *wasn't* a gay song.'

'Well,' Joan says, 'it could be a gay song, and it probably applies to gay people more than heterosexuals.' But it was written because of her observations, older people's reaction to public displays of closeness. And because of a general attitude she's noticed, almost a form of jealousy. 'When you see someone really happy with someone else you want them to be with you, and maybe get a little of that happiness.'

Joan made the same denial to Chris May, of *Black Echoes*, but added, 'I think people should be able to get on with what they want to do. It's down to that, as long as it doesn't hurt anybody else – as long as you know when to stop. As long as you don't start undressing and getting down to serious business! If you're walking down the street and you give your girlfriend a kiss and it's giving a lot of pleasure to one person then it shouldn't matter to other people that you're having a kiss.'

Joan's unwillingness to talk about her personal relationships is of a piece with her general decision not to class herself with any identifiable group, whether by race, gender or sexuality. She presents herself as a person, not a political animal, and the strength revealed in her work is both personal and universal. Her important statements are made in songs, not interviews, and we have to be content with that.

Joan makes very few gender references in her songs – it is very seldom 'he' or 'she', nearly always 'you' and 'me'. It may be simply that the feelings Joan expresses in her songs are so personal that a third-person reference would be inappropriate. But whatever the reason, the fact that sexuality is largely irrelevant to her writing is proved by the extraordinary way her songs appeal to and seem to speak equally to and for all sexes. Nevertheless, it must be noted that on the rare occasions when Joan *is* specific, the relationship is always with a man. But if we have to seek hard for hidden references at least gay people have had a lot of practice!

'What Do You Want' is back to the acoustic sound of the first two albums, but recorded with the experience of the intervening years. 'Wishing' in contrast is very seventies, through-composed operatic, starting with a strong dose of Joan's favourite blues and working its way through a selection of heavy rhythms.

'I wanted to write about wishing without actually saying what the thing was. That's the first bit of poetry I've ever written, and I had to rearrange it for the song.'

'Let It Last' starts with country music like The Band, then moves into strong swung gospel with Red hammering out the upper octaves. The two verses of this song are all about 'getting up/ To get kicked down', then the chorus challenges, 'I got no use for you if you're/ Only out to treat me unkind'. Which could all be said to a lover, or to a friend, but sounds like a challenge thrown out to the world, and the gospel ending turns it into a hymn – 'Let it last forever/ Until we die'.

While the album was being processed from master tape to packaged vinyl, Joan and the band were off on tour again. She returned to Britain in July for two events – one unfortunate, the other triumphant.

Joan had been commissioned to write and record the theme song for the British film *The Wild Geese*, an undistinguished adventure piece about a group of white mercenaries (with a token black) rescuing a deposed African president (Winston Ntshona) imprisoned by a corrupt dictator. The film is a tasteless exercise in commercialism and attracted controversy because of its perceived racialist implications. Unfortunately Joan failed to realize the kind of project in which she was involved, despite insisting on seeing a 'rough cut' of the film beforehand.

At the première she was heckled by a young crowd, shouting something to the effect that a self-respecting West Indian girl shouldn't be selling her ass by writing the theme song to a movie about mercenaries killing blacks. Interviewed the following afternoon, she said, 'Those people couldn't have seen the film – they just heard it was blacks getting killed and ...' she shrugged, with a nervous laugh. 'Well, they *are* killing blacks, and they *are* doing it solely for money, but the point they're trying to make is that they get double-crossed and they realize they're wrong and they got to live together and all this business. There's a big *moral*. I'm not saying it's a big deal – but it's a Boys Own film in terms of adventure, and there's a lot of fighting and it's *very* gory. But there is a message or moral, if you like – that we're all equal and should be able to live together.'

Joan's song itself, 'The Flight Of The Wild Geese' (produced by David Anderle), is a slightly mournful mid-tempo, piano-based number with more orchestration than it really needs. She tries to develop the moral she saw in the story, from considering rescue and escape to suggesting some sort of reconciliation: 'There's so much to be done – What more can we do?'

The other event this month was altogether more glorious, and one Joan remained proud of for years. Bob Dylan was headlining a festival at the Blackbushe Aerodrome in Hampshire, and had particularly asked for Joan Armatrading. 'Special guest' was Eric Clapton, with Graham Parker supporting. Joan certainly regarded this as an honour – 'I couldn't turn that down, could I! Apparently he's told lots of people he loves my work. Funny but I've never been a great Dylan fan. I like some songs but I'd be lying if I said he was my idol. *Blood On The Tracks* was the first Dylan album I got. That was very late, I know, but then I wasn't an early fan of anybody.'

Huge hydrogen balloons were gently bumping each other in the warm afternoon sun as Joan walked jauntily on to the stage dressed in muted Rastafarian colours. She had a largely new band – Bill Ham, Steve Bentley and Matt Betten on guitar, bass and drums, joining Red Young and Quitman Dennis. This outfit was quieter and more attentive to the songs, and Joan's performance was low key, making no concessions to the size of the event. However, after a confident 'Down To Zero', Red Young's delicate electric piano led into 'Help Yourself' and Joan proved that even a murmur could galvanize a crowd of two hundred and fifty thousand – 'If you're gonna do it/ Do it right'. Later, when Red took a sparkling piano break, she strolled to the side of the stage and leant against the PA stack as if it was a street corner, waving, swaying her hips and smiling in enjoyment of her band.

Significantly, perhaps, she did not play 'Flight Of The Wild Geese' but with a confident 'Here's the song you've been waiting for all day!' introduced 'Love And Affection'. She closed with 'Get In The Sun' and 'Mama Mercy' – no encore as the festival schedule was too tight.

To The Limit came out in September to the usual glowing reviews and in due course rose to number thirteen in the British charts. After the success of *Joan Armatrading* everyone had rushed out and bought *Show Some Emotion*, taking it to number six, but now Joan was back to her steady, passionate but finite body of fans. In promoting the album she did the usual round of interviews, though this time she was opening up a little more – again to a woman journalist. *Melody Maker*'s Penny Valentine was actually invited to Joan's Surbiton home, giving us a rare glimpse of her life away from stage and studio.

'You wouldn't think I was a good cook, would you?' she asks with a self-effacing smile, standing in her dungarees, stars-and-stripes braces pulled off as she works. She was chopping broccoli, carrots and chives fresh from her garden. They ate the vegetarian meal out of bowls with chopsticks, round the kitchen table. The house is large and rambling, old paint stripped to natural wood, soft pine furniture, windows thrown open onto a walled garden. A magnolia tree bursts into bloom outside the front door. In the garage sits an antique yellow and black Triumph sports car. Joan has lived here for a year, doing the place up herself. It is the first home she has ever owned, giving her a kind of freedom.

'I don't think of it like committing myself. Perhaps – if I was in a marriage situation ... but I'm not about to start a family and settle down. No, it's just somewhere I like, I can fix up the way I like, that's my own.'

After Joan has washed the dishes they leave the kitchen for the interview. As in the photos Annie Liebovitz took here for the album cover, Joan relaxes on the sofa, almost unguarded, laughing and frank by turns. In the room the television is tuned to *Coronation Street*, the sound turned down. The record collection – depleted a year ago by thieves – is fronted by the benign face of Tony Hancock. On the bookshelves *Star Trek* paperbacks jostle with Rita Mae Brown's *Rubyfruit Jungle*.

'You'd better like this album,' she says. 'I think it's the best I've ever done. Oh ... I suppose *that* means nobody else will think so.' Once again she insists that the songs are not personal. 'Even less so than usual. On the other albums there has always been the odd personal song, but here – definitely not. They're all ... um ... from what other people have said to me, or what I've seen.' And she relates 'Your Letter' and 'Barefoot and Pregnant' to the singer and to her agent.

Now she is prepared to admit that she had written about her own experiences in the past. 'I used to at one point, but I was never comfortable doing it. I'm not that sort of person. If you went and asked my mum she'd tell you. I've always been closed up. My family don't know the first thing about me. I've never been a person who tells what's happening.

'And when I did write about myself it all came out a mess because it was easy to write it, but it was hard to see it written. So I'd change things and that made it very confusing to people listening.' Joan had taken a break from writing after *Show Some Emotion*, feeling she wanted to do something different with this album, musically and lyrically.

She gave Penny Valentine a lift home after the interview. 'On the way we stop at a garage and Joan gets petrol and goes to the cash desk to pay. Sauntering across the courtyard in dungarees that stop just short of her ankles, a Michael Jackson tweed cap, her hands thrust deep into her pockets, she is, just for a moment, a defiant young kid from the block.'

Apart from interviews Joan took the rest of the year easy. She had decided not to tour for this album – 'Although I don't think anyone gets in the position of not doing *anything* when they've got a new album coming out. But I just fancied a rest after this past year. I don't really want to fall down on stage.'

When Joan was asked if she ever felt caught up in a process she couldn't control, she said, 'Nah – listen, you can always stop. Nobody *makes* you do anything. If things get too much you can say, "Thank you – I've had enough." If I felt at any point that I didn't like what was happening, and there was no way I could say, "I don't wanna do this," it's so easy – I just stay at home. It's no problem. I'll still have my two hands and I'll still be able to walk and breathe, and hopefully have my health. That's all that really matters.'

So Joan lived quietly at home avoiding parties and the sort of clubs and restaurants that 'remind me of who I am or what's going on. I'm on my own a lot, but I could count on one hand the times I've been lonely. It seems that if you always need people around it's a deficiency in you – if you need to be with them, not because they like you but because you don't like yourself. I'm happy with myself. But of course, there's always room for improvement!

'I have a good relationship with my two younger brothers and a sister but I don't really see much of the rest. My parents still live in Birmingham.'

Joan's favourite recreation then – as now – was comics. 'I buy the comics every week, just save them up. Fans have started to give me old ones, really different ones, weird things I've never heard of, some African ones. But I stick to the English ones.' What was the interest? 'Why, all human life is there!'

In December Joan gave a relaxed interview to Chris Thomas of *Black Echoes*, talking about the role of a producer. 'You definitely need someone outside. You need a producer and you need a manager too. Apart from anything else, you need someone to say, "OK – that's it, that's enough!" I can go to Glyn with a song that's written and finished and he'll be able to look at it and tell me it's too long. You might not realize until you're told because you're too close to it. He can tell me it could be better slower, faster, without that guitar solo. Just that little extra input can make all the difference. I trust Glyn totally. He knows what he's doing. Obviously there are times when he'll suggest something and there's no way I'm going to do it – so I just don't. But that doesn't happen too often. He's so good because he always knows what

93

to say, when to say it, and how to say it. He is the best producer I have ever worked with.'

She wouldn't want to produce herself. 'Maybe I wouldn't mind producing somebody else but I can't see me producing Joan Armatrading. I don't ever want to. Sometimes Glyn goes on at me because he doesn't understand the words on a particular track in the studio – like "Taking My Baby Up Town". I don't like to think that I write rubbish, and I do want people to hear what I'm saying, but at the same time I tend to concentrate more on the music and the rhythm of what I'm saying rather than the actual words. So I'd rather you didn't understand a word I said but felt that it fitted in with the music and the rhythm.'

She wouldn't be drawn on her plans. 'I know where I'd like to go,' she chuckled, 'but I don't want to tell you my ideas because if I don't do it I'll be disappointed to have seen it in print. So I'll just carry on and hopefully I'll do what I'm trying to do, and if it works out I'll be very happy.'

Early 1979 Europe was still snow- and ice-bound as Joan undertook her next world tour. The new band was also all-American. Red Young was retained on keyboards, but otherwise everyone was new: Richie Hayward from Little Feat on drums, Bill Bodine on bass, Ricky Hirsh guitar and Lon Price sax and flute. The band were more punchy, and – as in the studio – Joan felt inclined to give them the space they deserved.

'When I go on stage I never try and perform the songs as they are on record. I always try and put something new into them, mainly for my benefit, but also to keep the musicians and the audience interested. Quite often I rearrange a song so that it's totally different. I like to give the lads their freedom to express themselves so they're not bogged down playing the same thing all the time.'

New Musical Express reporter Graham Lock interviewed Joan at the Munich Hilton, a favourite with touring musicians. Asking her about her early support from the Women's Movement he got a short answer.

'I was never involved with feminism.'

'But didn't you do benefit gigs for *Spare Rib*?'

'Not *gigs*. I did one gig, and only did it because I knew somebody on *Spare Rib* and they asked me. I didn't do it for the Movement, I did it for a friend. I wasn't trying to say anything.... If the Women's Movement wanted to ... sort of adopt me, then I think that's great.

The music is there for everyone – men or women, gay or straight, or whatever. I love it when they like it.'

Joan was vociferous in her condemnation of the National Front, but wouldn't work for Rock Against Racism or the Anti-Nazi League.

'I think they're great, but it's something that needs dedication. Ian Dury said, if every person in the world sorted themselves out, this world would be great. It's the only way. You can try 'n' do your bit. I don't say I've got it all together, but I have a go.'

'Apart from your singing,' asked Graham, 'what do you mean by "doing your bit"?'

'Well ... it's like, for example, by living peaceably with somebody, like a black person and a white person. Then it's saying, OK, white people and black people *can* do it. Then you can do your bit without actually joining the gang.'

In March the British leg culminated in two gigs at Wembley Arena, a bold and possibly foolhardy choice of venue, probably prompted by Joan's success at Blackbushe. This cavernous hangar was hardly suited to Joan's style, but she still held the crowd and most of the critics spellbound for ninety minutes.

This time there was no new record to promote – Joan was in dispute with her record company. She was sueing A&M in the American courts, alleging that they illegally interfered with her attempts to negotiate for a new label. A variety of damages were listed totalling over ten million dollars. A&M maintained that Joan was still under contract to them, and they were granted an interim injunction by an English court restraining Joan from recording for any other company. Thus deadlock ensued with Joan refusing to record for A&M. Eventually the dispute was resolved amicably and discreetly, Joan staying with A&M, and neither party disposed to talk about the case.

Possibly as a result of the hiatus, no studio album was recorded or released this year, but in October a live album, *Steppin' Out* was issued, recorded by Glyn Johns on the American leg.

We plunge straight into the infectious rhythm of 'Mama Mercy', a touch funkier live and with some unusual stops, but otherwise a straightforward account – a good warming-up opener. Joan seems to be pacing her voice, but we still get the thrilling falsetto phrases.

'This next one needs no introduction –' 'Cool Blue Stole My Heart' is a surprise – a *laaazy*, slinky version, which immediately conjures up the 'hot sun' of the song, and the awakening of a holiday in Amsterdam five years ago.

'How Cruel' is new, destined for the B-side of 'Rosie' next year. Joan announces, 'Oh how cruel to make the girl cry – me!' and the keyboard takes us into the punky beat. This is Joan's first song to mention colour, and she goes straight to the point.

'How Cruel's where I say, Some people say, "She's too black" and some people say, "She's not black enough." No that's just a song about – anything you do, for some people will never be right. Which-ever way you go they wait for you to turn in a direction so that they can say you're wrong. . . . It was about people saying, "Why don't you write black music?" And then other people saying, "You shouldn't write black music." '

'Love Song' follows, which is only found on this album. It is a lilting ballad with no drums, which shows how 'Words seem to fail me, can't get to tell you, I . . . What I mean is . . . That is to say . . . I really do' – but 'I love you' is never said.

'Love And Affection' again produces that thrill with the quizzical opening discord. It is performed and sung with complete conviction, slowly, as Joan explores the gospel rhythm of the vocal line.

Side two opens with Joan's guitar, her solo version of 'Steppin' Out'. 'You Rope You Tie Me' proves a powerful and atmospheric live number which *segues* into a lyrical but urgent account of 'Kissin' And A Huggin' ', featuring several tasty solos including a too-brief snatch of bass. A soulful, triumphant 'Tall In The Saddle' completes the set. Some fans may regret the absence of 'Willow', but with Joan handing over vocals to the audience, this theatrical experience was best left for the video (*Track Record*) to capture.

With a band of this calibre, performances of such commitment and fresh insight as Joan gives, plus two interesting new numbers, this is a live album which easily earns its place in the collection.

Joan continued touring until the end of the year, only stopping when she fell ill in Australia and had an operation to have a cyst removed. She took three months to recuperate and took advantage of the time to think about new songs.

February 1980 brought a new single – apart from 'Flight Of The Wild Geese' (1978), her only single not to come off an album since 'Lonely Lady' in 1973. 'Rosie' is a bouncy, commercial-sounding number – with the most unlikely subject. 'Awe Rosie,' Joan begs, 'don't you do that to the boys. . . .' Rosie is a transvestite – 'Struttin' down the alley ways/ With the nervous young hopeful at his heel/ And he knows his satisfaction won't drive him away'. It's a very celebratory song, completely opposite in mood to Pink Floyd's 'Arnold Lane' or even The Kinks' defiant but panicky 'Lola'. In Britain the single reached number forty-nine, though it was a hit in Australia, a country where Joan came to feel very much at home.

The B-side is 'How Cruel' which Joan had introduced on tour. Both numbers were recorded in America, and both were produced by Joan herself, alone for 'Rosie' and with Henry Lewy on 'How Cruel'. Henry has worked with Joni Mitchell and Joan Baez. 'How Cruel' has the directness and simplicity of a demo or a commercial punk record. 'Rosie' with its infectious reggae beat does not attempt the polished sound of a Glyn Johns production but is entirely successful in conveying the good humour of the song. Joan had made her decision: she was making a complete break. The next album would be recorded in New York with an American producer, a new band and a direct approach.

'I've done three studio albums with Glyn. I just wanted to hear a different sound. I knew how I wanted to do it. It's like changing musicians – not because you've lost respect for the players. It's just that you sometimes have to get the person that suits the song – it's like moving on.'

TEN

All the way from America

The Midem Festival is the first music industry binge of the year – spring on the Mediterranean. In 1980 A&M hired a yacht for the business of entertaining, and American producer Richard Gottehrer was invited to a reception to meet Derek Green. After the usual chat Derek said, 'We have an artist we'd like you to do.'

'This was right after the Blondie successes,' Richard explains, – *Blondie* and *Plastic Letters* – 'so I assumed it would be a Blondie-like ...! And Derek said, "We'd really like you to do a record with Joan Armatrading!"

'I knew of Joan of course, and I was rather surprised at the time, but I thought it was a great opportunity and a great challenge for me. I loved the idea of doing it.'

When he returned to New York, Joan called on him briefly on her way home from California. 'She stopped in at my apartment to meet and we played the music and that was it. She had a tape of some songs.'

'When I got together with Richard,' says Joan, 'I didn't know anything about him really. We just talked. I was pretty confident in what I wanted, and in talking to him I was also pretty confident that he was going to help me get what I wanted. So that worked out pretty well.

'This was just a very easy album to write. All the songs were written in under an hour and "When You Kisses Me" in only ten minutes – in the hotel in New York the night before we did it. When I was ill I had a lot of time to really *think* about what I'd write and to jot down quite a few words. And I had a lot of ideas saved up. I knew pretty much the style of the songs I wanted to do. So I'd prepared it in my mind without going to the guitar or the piano. Once I felt well enough to get up and start it was all there and it just came out.'

Joan had made a definite attempt to keep the ideas simple and accessible.

'She always kept her eyes open and liked rock music and the combination of the elements,' says Richard. 'I think when someone suggested me, she liked the Blondie records or other things I'd done, so I think she was open for a change. The attitude of the arrangements, and to the music and the musicians I put together for her influenced the way that the record came out in a much more rock fashion.

'Listening to her earlier records, I liked them, but felt they weren't quite as focused round the individual songs. When you make a rock or a pop record you think out the elements a little differently. It's not such free-form playing – not that it's rigid of course, but you just think of where you want the hooks to come, where the solos should happen, and where you place the emphasis on the beat and the voice. Instead of surrounding it with a lot of music you pare it down and make the song and the singer important, and you make the music the element that builds it.'

The other vital element was the musicians, and Richard chose them carefully. He had been recording Robert Gordon with a young and relatively unknown drummer, Anton Fig, who went on to become one of the leading drummers in America. For those sessions Richard brought Chris Spedding (guitar) over from England.

'Chris is one of the best musicians available. He's unique and interesting and he finds different ways of doing things, so I built a lot around him. Then I researched other people that I thought might be sympathetic to Joan's music.' He assembled the basis of a variable studio band – 'different bands for different cuts,' as Anton puts it. Each track would be recorded as a 'live' performance, then reworked or added to as required. Extra musicians included Danny Federici and Clarence Clemons (organ and sax) of the E Street Band, and Joan brought in her band guitarist Ricky Hirsh.

Record Plant was a low-key studio on 44th Street on the west side, and fashionable in the seventies with such diverse customers as John Lennon and Kiss. It was a long, rectangular room with small partitions at the corners for the keyboards and guitar amps. The whole room was carpeted except the last five or six yards in front of the control room, where the wooden floor was left bare for the drums. Anton Fig set up with his back to the control room window, facing the rest of the band in the room. The drums were close-miked with an overhead room-mike for ambience.

Richard had picked some of the top session names in New York and Anton, the young rock drummer, was very conscious of his position. But Joan – the shy black woman over from England – appeared to slip into things easily enough.

'You know when you play with a good artist,' says Anton, 'you don't think of them in terms of gender. I was so much in awe of being in the session that I was coping with my own things anyway! I know she is a very shy person so it probably wasn't easy for her, but the sessions were going smoothly and she seemed to be enjoying herself.'

Joan had some of the songs on tape, some she played live on guitar or piano. As usual they seemed to emerge piecemeal, but Joan had a clear idea of how they should go.

'I'm pretty sure they were complete in her mind,' says Anton. 'They went really easily. I don't remember the sessions being that long, and I think that we recorded them as the songs came up – we learnt them and recorded them. There were no click tracks and we just played.'

Richard Gottehrer was a producer with a light touch. 'If he hears something that sounds good to him,' says Anton, ' then he'll pop up and say, "That's good!" More in the background than creating the stuff in his image.' Joan found him 'a very easy man to work with if you know what you want'.

'Joan played acoustic guitars,' says Richard. 'I put background voices on, early data synthesizers, all these things that were coming up. We used a small orchestra on "All The Way To America", and on "Turn Out The Lights" I got a soul background group.

'It was interesting, we became good friends at the time – she's actually quite a charming, funny person with a great sense of humour. She is shy – reserved - but she did relate to the musicians. She's the kind of person that'll do anything, but she does it best when she builds a rapport with people and a respect. I think that came across – we were family.

'I think Joan, being shy, she was also modest. I don't know if she really realized how good she was. She might even think that she wasn't a very good singer, and she was always working on her songwriting. There was never an air of cockiness or confidence. She was a very level-headed, reserved person with a lot of dignity. She was uncomfortable dealing with a lot of people in a new environment, but it took her some time and she warmed up. Maybe over the last few years she's achieved the feeling that she can do anything, but I think at the time it was still a building process for her. I think the record that we did was almost a turning point, it taught her the things she could accomplish that before she felt were beyond her reach.'

As well as the commercial rock numbers, Joan again tried her hand at reggae – 'Feeling In My Heart' and 'Simon' being two different examples. She had been on holiday in the West Indies, 'and there was lots more calypso than I thought there would be. There's lots of reggae. They were really good. I did reggae things even earlier that didn't get on albums, and there's reggae on *Show Some Emotion* and *To The Limit*.'

By now America was catching up with this music that had first made itself heard in Britain. Richard Gottehrer had spent three months in Jamaica working with Bob Marley and Lee Perry on an album for Martha Velez. Anton Fig had done a session with Garland Jeffreys, who had given him a pile of reggae records to listen to before the session.

For the final ballad, 'I Need You', Joan sang at the piano, then a string quartet was dubbed in and the piano track dropped.

'I really like that song,' Joan admits. 'Everybody really liked it. And when we started to do it Chris Spedding said, "This song is so beautiful" – that's the word he used – "you should have a string quartet on it." And straight away, you know, me and Richard Gottehrer, we just said, "That's it!" '

All in all this was a very enjoyable album for everyone concerned, and Joan stayed friendly with them. Whenever she is appearing in New York they go along. 'It was great,' says Anton. 'She is a quiet person, quite direct and very honest. I always found it very easy to get along with her, but I think a lot of stuff was unspoken.'

After the day's recording Richard would take Joan out to sample

Manhattan's food. 'I introduced her to some wonderful things that she had never had. There was one particular restaurant where she really enjoyed *cappulini frutti di mare*, which to this day is still a favourite of hers. And I introduced her to the fabulous spicy shrimps from Vincent's Clam Bar in Little Italy. She loves spicy food. These were two things that were unknown to her before her involvement with me and this record, and probably when it's all said and done they'll be the things that last!'

Richard is selling the pair of them short, of course. *Me Myself I* is a wonderful album and it gave Joan her highest ever chart placing at number five.

Joan is grinning on the cover, full-length photo, relaxed, and the mood of this album is more up-beat than anything before. The title track is exuberant – Joan is both rejoicing in her love of solitude and sending it up. This album is full of swagger and cheerfulness, and yet not short of poetry. Joan is singing out in full voice, abandoning the Glyn Johns close-mike technique for now.

In 'Ma-Me-O-Beach' she sends her colour up – 'I'm brown enough/ In fact/ I'm over done/ Turn me over'. Joan spotted the name on a signpost in Canada in the middle of nowhere, though she didn't go there. 'I bet it's just a lake or a little pond!'

With 'Friends' we are back on more familiar Armatrading territory as she remembers the ups and downs of an intense friendship, but her approach is still very positive, as is the musical feel. The drums are also loud on 'Turn Out The Light', a ballad in the classic Joan Armatrading mould.

The other startling ballad is 'I Need You' with its plaintive string backing. This song must have sounded like 'It Could Have Been Better' (*Whatever's For Us*) with its original piano accompaniment, but the string quartet is much more effective than the blanket orchestration of the earlier album.

The soft reggae simplicity of 'Feeling In My Heart' contrasts with the restless, disorientating beat of 'Simon', which perfectly captures the twisted mentality of Simon's brother.

'I don't know who Simon is,' says Joan. 'I was just thinking in terms of two brothers, two people that I know and one of them always felt it wasn't right. I don't know, his mom loved the other one better, and he was always the ugly one. His brother was more intelligent than he was. Then it's just a matter of making up a story, cos some of it was there.'

'All The Way From America' starts with an artless acoustic strum like any old sixties folk hit. There seem to be several rhythmic dislocations centring on the Duane Eddie style guitar twangs, but unlike Joan's earlier records everything fits exactly into straight 4/4 bars. It's one of the most tuneful of Joan's songs – yet it only got to number fifty-four.

'It's just about somebody who phones up from America and says, "Hang on, I'll be there in a minute, and probably we'll get married," or whatever. But all they did was phone once, maybe twice, and then they didn't phone again. And you're just left there hanging on with all this great promise of whatever, you know, and nothing happens. And then you just decide, "Well, I've had enough, I'm not waiting around." '

The album raced up the charts and Joan kicked off another world tour in Europe with substantially the same band as last year (and the live album): Ricky Hirsh, Bill Bodine and Richie Hayward again on guitar, bass and drums, plus Dickie Simms from Eric Clapton's band on keyboards and an extra guitarist in Rick Beilke. There was no sax player this time.

'The band was such fun on stage,' Joan recalls. 'You don't really have to smile to show you're enjoying yourself. I would look around and either you would get a big grin or just see that they were into it as well. It helps when you seem to be enjoying it, the audience seems to enjoy it more, so it's just a circle feeding back. It's really good.'

In June the single 'Me Myself I' went to number twenty-one and the world tour was followed by another British tour in October. Joan's relaxed mood was glimpsed at the Birmingham Odeon when, after the show, she came racing up the aisle to greet a relation before the audience had even cleared from the hall.

Earlier in the year, between tour dates, Joan had retreated to her home in Kingston with some new toys. Encouraged by the success of the album she had bought a Prophet keyboard and a Linn drum-machine and got busy making a very different demo tape from anything she had done before. Now she could produce something that sounded like a complete band all by herself. She could add vocals in the privacy of her home and wouldn't have to strum through new songs to a circle of musicians in the studio – she could simply play them the tape.

In fact Joan had decided to go even further. She had always had firm ideas of how her songs should go, and this time she intended to play a larger part in realizing them. She believed it would be possible to make an album using only a drummer and a lead guitarist. She would play everything else herself.

So Joan returned to New York with her demo tape to record the next album with Richard Gottehrer.

'The second album came about,' he says, 'because the first one did so well. Joan came in with these finished demos and they were good. They were done with machines and we tried to duplicate them with musicians. She specifically asked for Anton Fig on drums and Chris Spedding on guitar.'

'I felt it was a great honour,' Anton says, 'that she had felt comfortable enough with me and liked my playing enough to ask me to play on another record with her.'

He remembers that in some instances he actually added drums to her demos, playing along with the pre-recorded tape. 'It was an almost completed tape in some instances,' he says. 'I don't think all the songs were like that, but some of them were.'

When they were recording a song from scratch Joan now played her Prophet keyboard in the studio in preference to her old acoustic guitar.

Richard Gottehrer was worried about these changes. 'I always thought that we should get the same musicians and expand on them and go to the next level of what we'd done – you know, just do it even better. We'd already sold over a million records and I really thought she was onto something. What happened on the second record was – it was in the early days of electronics and I think Joan really wanted something else out of it, and it just didn't happen. We did it and it was kind of stilted, I thought. There was a stiffness about it. Joan wanted to play almost everything herself – like any true artist you change a lot. She had done one thing – she wanted to do something else.

'So it was up and down, but I thought it was OK. What we did was good. Some things were better than others. I thought we were more on track with "No Love", which I thought was a great song.'

A&M thought differently, however, and reluctantly turned the album down.

ELEVEN

When I get it right

It would have made sense for Joan to go back into the studio and remake the album with Richard Gottehrer, but this didn't happen. 'Probably after doing it the first way,' he says, 'she just wanted to go home, and that's what she did.'

Fortunately for Joan and A&M, someone was waiting in the wings. An up-and-coming young British producer had approached A&M to suggest he might work with Joan. Steve Lillywhite had made his name with Peter Gabriel, Ultravox, XTC, Siouxie and the Banshees, Eddie and the Hot Rods and U2. 'And A&M seemed to think it was a good idea.' They arranged for Steve and Joan to meet.

Joan played Steve a couple of tracks from the New York tape – 'once only, and wouldn't let me take a tape away. I realized I had to get some good musicians in, so I basically pulled in a few of the players I'd worked with on Peter Gabriel's album.'

So two Americans, Jerry Marotta and Tony Levin, formed the basis of the strong rhythm section which was the foundation of this album. They recorded at the Town House, the Chiswick studio where Steve was based. He used the drum room to get the big sounds for which he was famous. But unlike his usual procedure of first recording drums and bass, Joan chose to put down the basic tracks with a four-piece band, just as she had done from the beginning. So she played acoustic guitar and they brought Nick Plytas in on keyboards – usually organ or piano. Steve was surprised she didn't play piano herself. 'It's funny. She loves playing guitar. It's not so much that she doesn't want to play the piano, it's more that she wants to play the guitar.'

So with this rhythm-section line-up they re-recorded the songs Joan had first done in New York. Steve soon took to this way of working as it produced excellent results. 'She really loves playing with other musicians and being out there. But she will never do a vocal, not even a guide vocal, along with the musicians. She might play them the demo which has a guide vocal on. I remember that she wouldn't let anyone see her singing either. We had to put a big screen up and she'd be on the other side.'

As in the past, the lack of guide vocals sometimes made it difficult for the musicians, though the songs on this album were much more regular than her earlier ones. They had been written with a drum-machine so the bar lengths tended to be regular. But as Steve says, 'She always likes throwing in the odd bar. Playing it is more difficult than you think sometimes. I don't know why she throws those in – just to keep people on their toes, I would think!'

And Joan does like to keep people on their toes. 'She opened up to the musicians as it went along. But they were actually scared stiff of her to start off! Part of my job is to make a really nice atmosphere for the musicians to perform properly.' Joan didn't feel it was her job though, and she used to growl at them. But as the sessions turned out well she mellowed and opened up to them. 'But at the end when they'd all come up and say, "Great, Joan! Really enjoyed it!" she would just mutter, "All right. Bye."'

Two musicians were treated to a little more respect, however – the Jamaican drummer and bass player Sly Dunbar and Robbie Shake-speare. Steve recalls, 'There was a reggae track ["I can't Lie To Myself"] that we thought would be really good if we could get Sly and Robbie, and we booked them. Very much gangsterish – they arrived, they wanted £600 each – in cash – used notes – on the day! She was quite impressed with them, actually more because they were black, I think. But they were just as cool as her!' And he laughs.

Once the basic tracks were down it was time to add the synthesizer, which would make this album sound very different from all her previous ones. It was to be her first real step into the eighties. So far keyboards had formed part of the texture of the band, but on the demos for this album Joan had come up with strong musical lines, like the opening riff on the first track, 'I'm Lucky'. She had written such lines into several of the songs and it had to be just the right person to play these. Joan had no one special in mind, so Steve got in touch with Thomas Dolby. They had known each other since Steve was a tape-op at Phonogram studios in the mid-seventies.

As Thomas recalls, 'She'd done a lot of the demos at home with a Linn drum-machine and a Prophet-5, and they were simplistic, but very interesting. It sounded like she was having fun with a new instrument, finding stuff that she never would have found on the guitar maybe – which I find myself, I hardly play the guitar, but if I sit down with the guitar I come up with stuff that I would never have come up with on a keyboard. And so a lot of the songs, for example, "I'm Lucky", she had a basic synthesizer riff that she played already. So they were looking for somebody who would play the parts well and program the best sound, and Steve, I guess, liked my playing and asked me to do it.

'I came into the studio and he played me a tape of her demo, and she would throw in a few comments here and there, but mostly it was Steve explaining what they were trying to do. It was a time when an awful lot of people were messing around with electronics for the first time, and there was a good atmosphere generally in the business then for experimentation. Certainly people were feeling they should be moving away from just a band sound and branching out.'

He set up his keyboards in the control room.

'I used Joan's own Prophet because it had some of the basic library sounds in that she'd used on the demos, which I played around with and polished up a bit.'

He also used a couple of his own instruments. 'My workhorses at the time were a Micro-Moog and a Roland JP4, which was quite modern at the time.'

Thomas worked in the control room with Steve, Joan and the engineer, Steve Brown. When he joined them the basic tracks were already recorded.

'They sounded really great, the tracks – very spacious. And it was in the early days of that Town House/Stone Room sound Phil Collins had been messing with – gated reverb [big, short echo] and so on. Steve Lillywhite was the premier exponent at the time of that sound.

A lot of other people had either dry sounds or very long reverbs; they didn't really have that crunchy reverb sound. They were very interesting tracks to listen to just on their own. There might have been some rough strummed guitar which Joan had laid down, but with a lot of my tracks, especially the more central ones like "I'm Lucky" or "Eating The Bear", I was working with just drums and bass.'

Steve found himself explaining Joan's ideas to Thomas. 'A lot of the synth lines she'd written herself and were on the demo, and really *had* to be that way. Sometimes I think she goes a little too far in telling musicians what to do. Because sometimes they can maybe work out a better line than she does. Although the more we worked, I managed to convince her sometimes – she became a bit more pliable. But she's still very much her own person.'

Thomas found Joan 'quite insular'. He says, 'I'm not sure how much she liked a lot of what I did. There was inevitably some stuff that she liked, but sometimes she would say I was just playing something wrong. She would sing it to me or play it to me on guitar and I would play it as close as I possibly could, and I couldn't really see what I was doing wrong, but it would just be something in the way she heard the phrasing or the sound.

'She was very tense. I got the impression overall that the laborious process of layering of recording, she found a little bit hard, a bit frustrating. So she preferred to disappear and come back, and make comments. Sometimes she would go away for two hours and come back and say that was a part she didn't like, that we had just spent three-quarters of an hour on. But in a way I can sympathize with that, because if you spend three-quarters of an hour working on a sound or a part, you're automatically protective about it. Whereas if some-body has been away and they come back, they go, "What the hell is that? It sounds like a dying bumble-bee or something!" '

So while Steve and Thomas worked, Joan would disappear. 'There was a little room upstairs at the Town House which had a pool-table and Space Invaders machine. She would go and play that for hours – she had just caught the bug.'

'She never has any money,' says Steve. 'She's not mean but she looks after her money – and she was so addicted to Space Invaders that she couldn't handle the fact of taking money out of her pocket to put into Space Invaders, so she actually got the studio to provide her with a big bag of 10ps! Which obviously just went on the bill. But she couldn't handle putting her own – spending like £3 or £4 at a time on this game.'

On 'No Love' a string sound was needed, and in those days there were no 'sampled' strings. Real string sections had been used on several of Joan's albums, but Steve had cut his teeth on punk and this was the eighties, so it was up to Thomas to synthesize the sound.

'That was a combination of Prophet and JP4. In those days there was no midi [to link keyboards] so I'd have to play the same part, triads [three-note chords] on both keyboards at the same time and generally work on the two sounds together. There were a couple of tracks with strings and things on.'

'Only One' was the other song. 'Thomas Dolby did some good stuff on that,' Steve recalled. 'Joan gave him a bit of leeway to work round that.'

Steve and Thomas had no problems communicating. 'Steve'd just grin and say, "It's a bit thin, isn't it?" or "It's a bit buzzy", or "a bit dull", or "I liked that one you had five minutes ago!" It was divided between some parts that were fundamental to the composition which Joan had written for the demo, just perfecting and fine-tuning them, and then other things where he'd leave me pretty much to my own devices.

'Whenever I work for other people it's like a holiday from my own stuff. I always try and do the most different stuff from my own that I possibly can. Because when I walk into a session like that I'm very nervous – especially if my reputation has preceded me! I did enjoy it – but I found Joan a little bit inaccessible....

'I think it was a hard time for her also, because she was really branching out musically and she was worried about it. People were still quite suspicious of synthesizers in those days. So because it was an area that she didn't know that much about, she was worried that you'd be taking something away from her – taking something out of her grasp. Which incidentally, I found very much with Joni Mitchell as well, who is a keyboard player – it was like taking a toy away from a child. The moment I played a sound that was a little bit alien to her, it was kind of, "You're contaminating my record!" And over a period of time in both cases it was skating on thin ice.'

Thomas feels she was more relaxed with Steve. 'They seemed to have a good working relationship. She'd put her confidence in him – she'd given him the licence really to go ahead and guide her through a new way of working, and I think as such he had that security – he was the man hired for the job. I don't know how comfortable it was for him, but he certainly pulled it off very aptly.

'I remember a strange experience at the end. We finished late one night and I said, "It's too late to pick up my keyboards, I'll come back tomorrow." So the next day I came in to get my stuff, but nobody had told Joan I was coming in, and she was just setting up to do vocals. She had already thrown everybody out of the studio and put curtains all around the vocal booth so that not even Steve could see her. And got an array of drinks and a desk for her lyrics and things like this. I felt terrible because I had obviously interrupted this psyching-up process that she was putting herself through in order to do the vocal. But I also felt quite strange because she treated me very, very coldly. That's understandable, I guess, considering what had happened, and yet I thought that over the previous five days or whatever, although I wouldn't say we'd become *close* by any means, I thought, well, at least we're on friendly, open terms now. And then suddenly it seemed like I was a complete stranger – "What the hell are you doing in the studio?" '

Finally it came to the mixing, a process which interested Joan, though she didn't wallow in it. 'She employs people to do the job,' says Steve, 'and she'll say yes or no – she never takes a tape home. And she didn't like spending a long time mixing. It's not like three-day mixes which you now get people doing. We'd mix one or two a day, maybe. Joan was involved as much as any other artist. But people have their own talents, which is why she employs them. So what she doesn't know much about, she won't say things about – she's dead cool like that.'

Steve was very pleased with the album, as was Thomas.

'I felt that everything I'd done which was worth hearing was there, and was audible in the mix. The arrangements on that album are very sparse and you can hear everything that's going on. Whereas on some of her successive albums they got more rocky – after she'd been out touring the stadiums with a live band it got a lot more rock-'n'-roll and it was harder to distinguish individual parts. I like the space of that album.'

Walk Under Ladders was released in September and went to number six in the UK charts. 'I'm Lucky', the opening track (from which the album title comes) scraped in at number forty-six.

It is significant that this album is not called *I'm Lucky*. *Me Myself I* showed Joan rejoicing in confidence, in breaking away, flying to America. This album is the other side – the confidence to challenge and take risks. It opens strongly with a synthesizer riff, bold but in a minor key, despite the upbeat tone of the lyric. The next two songs, 'When I Get It Right' and 'Romancers', are about challenging what other people say about you, while 'I Wanna Hold You' is saying, I'll do it even if it's wrong – 'You're going out/ With someone /I don't approve of/ And it's getting me /In a state'. This is a new kind of (non) relationship for Joan to write about – though it has that element of friend/lover ambivalence which often appears.

'The Weakness In Me' is another of Joan's classic ballads, the aching intensity of the music matching the agony and indecision in the words. It is one of Joan's most pointed lyrics – 'Make me lie /When I don't want to /And make someone else/ Some kind of unknowing fool'. – and could also be a reply to the last song where the singer is threatening to break up a relationship.

'No Love' has Joan showing her strength again, saying no to a lover who is just not prepared to offer enough. 'At The Hop' is her wry, even sour, answer to all those cheerful fifties boppers (complete with Gary Sanford's 'Chuck Berry' guitar solo). Once again Joan and her baby are heading for the bright lights, this time to dance to a strident, ominous sound reminiscent of Bowie's *Scary Monsters* of the previous year.

Incidentally, early the following year Joan's first and only song-book was published (Rondor Music/Wise Publications/Music Sales). *The Best of Joan Armatrading* is fifteen songs from as early as 'Cool Blue Stole My Heart' through to four songs from *Walk Under Ladders*. The cover is by the artist Edward Bell, who did *Scary Monsters*, with a portrait in just the same style and with identical border and handwritten titles.

After Joan's previous experiments with reggae, 'I Can't Lie To Myself' builds on the real thing, with Sly and Robbie pacing the steady beat, but the lyric is decidedly lightweight.

'Eating The Bear' seems to be a clear metaphor for facing one's own fears – 'Some days the bear/ Will eat you/ Some days you eat the bear' – and Joan tackles this paranoia with confidence and humour. In some quarters the song became a libbers' anthem – which Joan thought was typical of the way people twisted her lyrics. 'You see, anybody can be the bear. It's not a knock at male aggression. If a bloke had written that song they wouldn't have said he was getting at women. Like I'm accused of writing too many songs about love as well, but if you listen to the radio nearly all the stuff is love songs. It's such a basic everyday human symptom that it's hard not to bring it in.'

'Only One' is an exercise in mood, again with a pretty inconsequential lyric, and rather an unsatisfying end to an important album.

Richard Gottehrer's opinion of this album is interesting. 'I know a lot of people like it, but I thought the versions of the material they did afterwards were not right. I don't really think that was a very good record, *Walk Under Ladders*.' Unfortunately we will never get a chance to make a comparison, but this is probably the natural perspective of someone who has been very close to the material and finds it hard to hear a different interpretation. Pete Gage and Gus Dudgeon, for example, both hated the production on each other's albums, although Gus was full of praise for Glyn Johns.

The usual round of interviews started and Joan was asked if she thought she had been left behind in the rush to the next fad. 'Well, I don't think people have actually forgotten me – I just think people might look at something else because it's a little more eye-catching. I mean, I really like Toyah and Ultravox, for example.'

Joan was now living in a modest, detatched house near Kingston-upon-Thames, Surrey. Her chief hobby was fishing for trout. She had given up eating meat. She also enjoyed 'driving around in my Honda, sightseeing.

'I'm a happier person nowadays, but I still don't know what success is. I sell a lot of records and get a good audience reaction at concerts, but I'm still striving for artistic achievement. The next song will always be the best.

'I still feel I'm serving an apprenticeship. I'm still working on finding out about myself and mentally I'm not much different from when I left home at the age of seventeen. The goal is still to write songs and lead a band in a studio, but mainly to improve on my songwriting. All

I want is to keep writing songs and be able to work with musicians who know how to play their instruments.

'Really, I'm a songwriter first and last. I'm shy and don't go much on the personality bit. I enjoy living through those songs. The gap [between writer and performer] has narrowed over the years, but not from my own choice. I used to be completely embarrassed about getting on stage, and still am sometimes. But it's obvious that people want to see the writer of the songs perform them, so I've slowly come to terms with it.'

But in another interview she was more upbeat. 'Playing live is becoming one of my favourite things. The last tour I played a lot of stand-up places which I like – it's good to see people moving around. Now I ask to play in unseated auditoriums wherever possible so that people can get up and dance. I'm still in love with music, though I know you can't trust people on the business side as much as I'd like to.'

Joan had a world tour booked to start in October, but a minor operation in London that month meant a postponement until December.

Thomas Dolby went along to see one of the shows at the Hammersmith Odeon. 'As I recall, Justin Hildreth who had been my drummer for some time got me a comp. I went in during the sound check and stood at the side of the stage and Justin came over and said hello to me. Joan called over to him and said, *"Justin!"* very sternly, like a governess or something, and didn't even bat an eyelid in my direction, which is a bit strange.'

A couple of hours later 'she was at the end of a walkway, dressed in white in a spotlight, with a mike, singing "Willow" unaccompanied, with a big grin from ear to ear on her face, in front of a couple of thousand people. That was very strange – I never quite felt that I could understand. . . .

'I think it takes an awful lot of digging for her to dig up the exhibitionist side of her nature in order to go out and do it. But it's a ten-year link to the world via her music, and I think she channels all her desire to communicate into that, and socially it's very hard for her to communicate, certainly with strangers. I think she's just a very private person.

'The odd thing was, although she was very frosty towards me, it didn't really put a dent in my respect for her. She was one of my heroes when I was a lot younger. Very often some of my other heroes from that era that I've met, it's taken a little magic out of my life, because you meet them and they're human and have human failings, and I feel afterwards that something has gone – a piece of the magic is missing. I didn't really feel that with Joan. I could enjoy one of her records as much now as I could before then, which is certainly not true for a lot of other people.'

TWELVE

Right on target

1982 was the first year there was no Joan Armatrading album released since 1974 (although 1979 saw only a live album after her dispute with A&M). This was not a particular lapse, it was rather that Joan was producing an album every year-and-so-many-months and 1982 just happened to fall in the middle of the period. Joan was touring, and a concert from Boston was televised on BBC 2.

She and Steve Lillywhite went into the Town House studio again, with Joan keen to have another try at doing more herself. 'She felt that again she would give it a go but not on the whole album.' This time Joan's ambition was to play guitars rather than keyboards. The only other musician was Stewart Copeland, now a world-class drummer with Police, who were also A&M artists, and managed by Stewart's brother Miles, Joan's ex-manager. Stewart had looked after Joan on her first solo tour of America way back in 1973. 'Tell Tale' was the track, and Joan played acoustic and electric guitar, and bass, but this was overdubbed by Tony Levin when the main album sessions began.

These took place in Abba's Polar Studio in Stockholm. 'Sweden was really nice,' Steve remembers. 'It's a pretty weird place really because half the year it's all light and half the year it's all dark. People are pretty weird.'

There were two studios at Polar. Joan's party worked in the big one

The front cover of *Sounds*,
25 December 1976.

Front cover of *What's On*, 13 June 1980.

BELOW: Joan's hobby is reading comics.

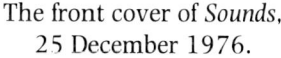

LEFT AND ABOVE: Publicity photos of Joan.

BELOW: Photo by Annie Liebovitz, taken in Joan's south London home, for the cover of *To The Limit*.

iecey Williams, p10; Eddie Henderson competition, p 11

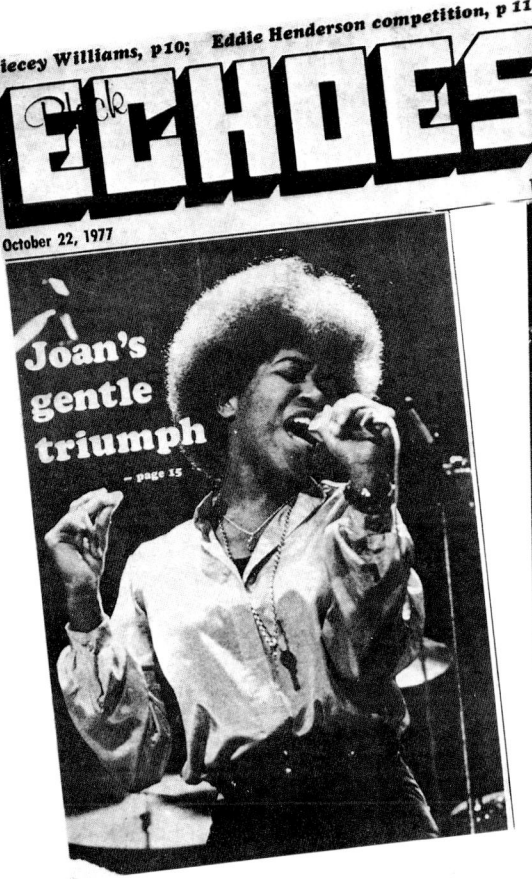

Black ECHOES

15p

October 22, 1977

Joan's gentle triumph

— page 15

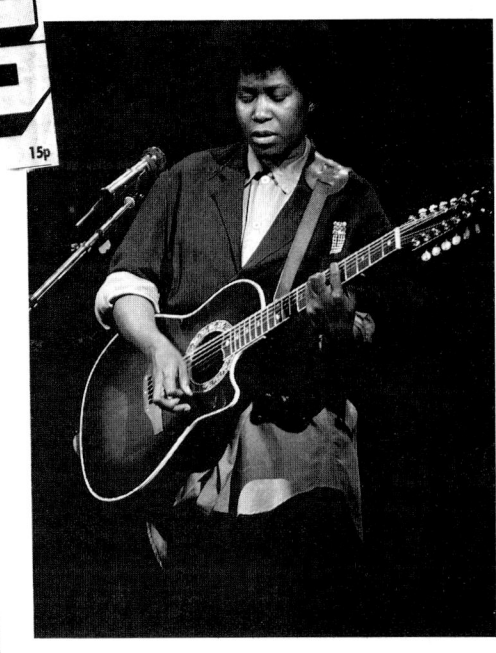

LEFT: Front page of *Black Echoes*, 1977.

ABOVE: Joan in performance.

BELOW: Joan meets the fans, New York 1980.

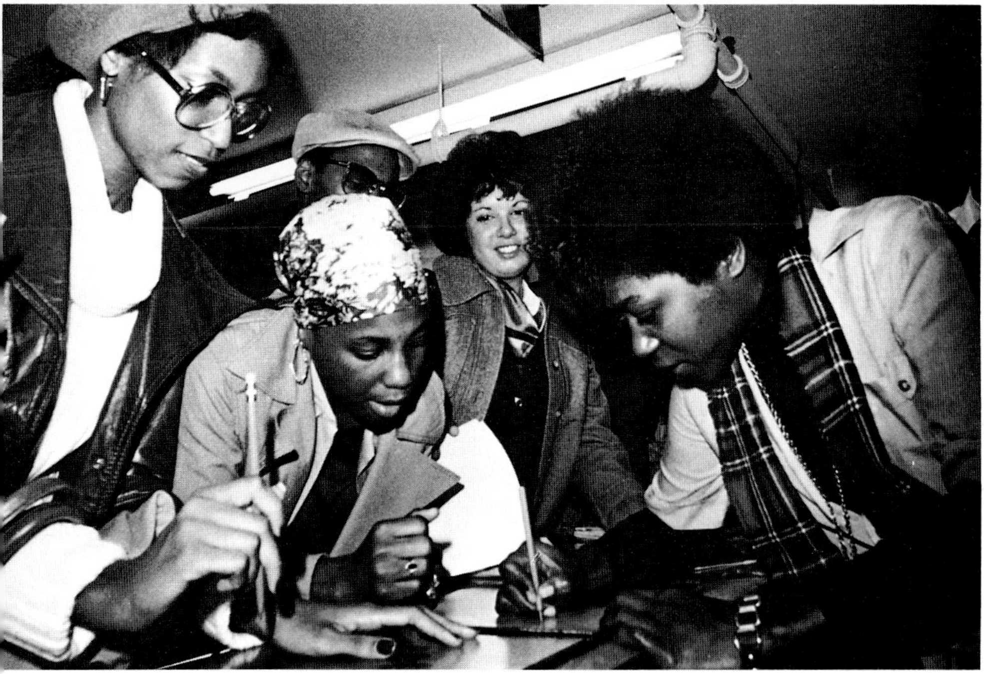

Melody Maker

SEPTEMBER 18, 1976   15p weekly   USA 75 cents

THIS is Joan Armatrading who, following the British chart success of her latest album, is currently trekking across America on a long club tour.

She has played many of America's most prestigious clubs, including the Roxy in Los Angeles, where she received rave critical applause. And last week Armatrading appeared at the Bottom Line in New York, a show reviewed by the MM's reporter in America, Chris Charlesworth, on page 20.

Joan breaks the tour next week for a special London concert at Hammersmith Odeon on September 23. The show is the prelude to a full-scale British tour during the first two weeks of December.

And she appears on BBC-2's Old Grey Whistle Test on October 5, accompanied by the band who have backed her in America — Dave Mattacks (drums), Jerry Donahue (guitar) and Pat Donaldson (bass).

Tangerine Dream tour

TANGERINE DREAM come to Britain this autumn, playing nine major provincial concerts as part of a long European tour.

The group release a new album, called "Stratosfear," on October 22. Tangerine Dream's first-ever single will also be available at the beginning of November.

The concerts start at EDINBURGH Usher Hall on November 3 and continue at MANCHESTER Free Trade Hall (5), COVENTRY Theatre (7), NOTTINGHAM Albert Hall (8), PORTSMOUTH Guildhall (9), CARDIFF Capitol (10), BIRMINGHAM Odeon (12), LEEDS University (13) and CROYDON Fairfield Halls (14).

All box-offices open this week, except for Croydon (open from October 1) and Leeds (November 1).

Tangerine Dream also appear in a BBC-2 film on October 3. The film, made by Tony Palmer, was shot during Dream's cathedral tour last October.

Melody Maker

JULY 15, 1978   15p weekly   USA 75 cents

CLASH talk on page 8
Moodies interview—page 10
Talking Heads A great album: p23

BOB DYLAN returns to Britain on Saturday for the climax to his European tour — his Picnic at Blackbushe for 100,000 adoring fans.

As well as promising a revised set from his six Earls Court shelves, the show offers fans the likelihood of Dylan jamming with his buddy Eric Clapton who plays with his band an support in Dylan after-sets by Merger, Lake, Joan Armatrading and Graham Parker and the Rumour.

The prospects of Clapton and Dylan playing together on stage has been fuelled by the burgeoning friendship between the two — a friendship sealed when they got together in Dylan's hotel room after his Nuremberg festival appearance last week and spent all night playing and writing songs.

On top of the changed Dylan set, other attractions are promised for the show — including a firework display and the record company CBS.

To tie in with Blackbushe, MM today presents a four-page supplement with all the fax in and about the festival that many fans see as the show of the year.

● On page 31 is a how-to-getthere guide complete with order maps and transport details.
● On page 32, Michael Gray reviews Dylan's show in Paris last Friday — a concert that gives a fair indication of what to expect at Blackbushe.
● Colin Irwin talks to Joan Armatrading, club's first lady a couple of years back, who was personally invited onto the Blackbushe bill by Dylan.
● On page 34 Chris Welch interviews Harvey Goldsmith, the promoter who brought Dylan to Britain: how he landed the gig, his rights to 96,000 people to see their fans, and why is the man behind the Blackbushe enterprise.

IT'S DYLAN'S PICNIC

BLACKBUSHE 4-page focus SEE PAGE 31

AFTER a year's absence, the Bay City Rollers returned to the stage in Britain last week — and were greeted by fan hysteria at the opening concerts in Scotland.

The tour opened in Dundee last Thursday, moving on to the band's hometown, Edinburgh, and then to Glasgow on Saturday, where tartan-clad teenybop fans clashed with police outside the Apollo.

In Manchester on Sunday, the Rollers' show before 4,000 fans at Belle Vue was stopped after the opening number when 20 young girls broke through security cordons onto the stage. The band returned to the dressing room until things cooled down.

The British tour, the first with new rhythm guitarist Ian Mitchell, may be the band's last in Britain. They have become a major chart act in America and no live there, because of the British tax laws, and manager Tam Paton claims, difficulties in finding British theatres prepared to stage the band.

Paton last week announced his engagement to year-old London student Marcella Knaflova. Pictured at their celebration in Manchester are (left to right) Les McKeown (vocals), Stuart Wood (bass), Mitchell (rhythm), Eric Faulkner (lead guitar) and Derek Longmuir (drums).
● Rollers on the road — page 8.

Joan, relaxed and on stage.

OPPOSITE ABOVE: Cartoon of Joan and the
Bob Dylan Blackbushe Picnic from *Melody
Maker*, 1978.

OPPOSITE LEFT: Front page of *Melody Maker*,
which hangs on Joan's studio wall.

FOLLOWING PAGE: Joan at New York Pier,
1984.

while Abba's 'Bennie and Bongo' as they called them, were working on the demos for *Chess* in the small studio. *The Key* was an enjoyable album to make, Steve getting to know Joan better, and her girlfriend also came out.

'She's really, really nice. She's an artist, and really down to earth. Whenever Joan plays London she always buys a ticket because – she could get one free, obviously, but, quite rightly saying, that you get a much better seat when you buy a ticket. So she's always first at the box office, buys a seat right in the front. Whereas all the freebies, you're always stuck at the back....'

This time Joan had demos for all the songs, and a few chord sheets, so she didn't have to perform them to the musicians in the studio.

'I've always had great fun working with her,' Steve says, 'because she'd always come in the studio well prepared.'

They used Jerry Marotta and Tony Levin again on drums and bass, and Darryl Sturmer (guitar) from Genesis' live band. Steve couldn't remember why, but they didn't use Thomas Dolby.

'Maybe Tom was too famous by this time – she often feels a little bit wary about that sort of thing. We got Larry Fast to come over. And Joan didn't actually like Larry Fast that much, because he was actually less of a player than Thomas Dolby. He'd worked with Gabriel a lot, he's far more of a boffin really, Larry. So I think she may have realized afterwards she should have asked Tom.'

Some of the synthesizer parts on the demo suggested brass, 'so we thought we might get real people in to do it.' Steve had never worked with brass before – 'I come from punk rock. I've only just recorded my first strings.' So he asked Mel Collins to put a team together. He played sax on *Walk Under Ladders* (and first met Joan on *Show Some Emotion*), and brought in Guy Barker and Annie Whitehead (trumpet and trombone) to complete the trio.

After experimenting on 'Tell Tale' Joan took the plunge and played electric guitar on half the tracks. She has never fully come to terms with the instrument, often attacking it like an acoustic, but submerging the sound in effects pedals. 'She's a bit like a kid in a sweet shop in that respect! She loves making noises.'

One of the last musicians to join them was Adrian Belew, whose extraordinary abilities had first surfaced when Frank Zappa had spotted him playing in his local Nashville rock club. David Bowie had 'poached' him from Zappa, and he had gone on to work with Robert Fripp.

'I'd always wanted to work with Adrian Belew – as did Joan,' says Steve. 'I think she almost wanted him on it because she wanted to find out how he made those noises! And it's just a Roland Chorus JC-120 and he just puts the guitar [against the amp]. The guitar that starts "I Love It When You Call Me Names", that was all him – that wasn't Joan's line at all.'

Adrian reports, 'I arrived at the studio exhausted from the flight, carrying my cases and looking forward to a rest. When Joan saw me she said, "Are you Belew?" and insisted I start right away. Towards the end of those sessions she was getting very friendly, trying to coax out of me how I get these sounds. I showed her, but I don't know if she can do it.'

Back in London, A&M decided that the album was short on really commercial songs, so Joan actually went away and wrote 'Drop The Pilot' and 'What Do Boys Dream'. These were produced in New York by Val Garay ('Bette Davis Eyes') with a different band entirely, much to Steve Lillywhite's chagrin.

'No, there was not much I could do about it because – for some reason I wasn't about, or A&M thought that she had to use "An American". I think I could have produced that really well. I mean, one of the favourite songs I ever did with her was "I Love It When You Call Me Names".'

Despite the album's overall confident sound, Steve didn't feel it was as good as *Walk Under Ladders*. It certainly had one track that let it down: ' "I Love My Baby" – give us a *break*, Joan! Sometimes her lyrics are terrible ... I'm afraid. She's written classic love songs, but "I Love My Baby" ain't one of them.'

Steve's general memories are, 'She *hates* people taking photographs. American session players especially, they come over with their *fantastic* cameras and they bring them down to the studio and want to take shots of everything and – *No cameras! No cameras!* In fact I remember one of her musicians telling me that once they were on tour and there was a press conference and there were lots of cameramen, press photographers there. And one of the band got his camera out and was in among the press photographers, and in front of everyone Joan went up, snatched his camera and really embarrassed this poor guy.

'So she has a reputation, if you don't know her, of being ... Well, you know her love of comics. She's actually got in her house *The Beano* framed – she actually was in *The Beano* once because she'd written to them and said how much she liked them and they'd written her into a story. One of the characters was going to a Joan Armatrading concert – so she's got that framed. It's either *Dandy* or *Beano*. She gets them all delivered to her house.

'She doesn't drink. She can't remember *ever* having a drink. She doesn't even drink tea or coffee. Hot water. I think chocolate's one of her vices.

'Let me see. She doesn't like smoking. I don't think she *minds* people smoking – have people smoked joints in front of her? Maybe once or twice. But it felt a bit naughty, you know. Any harder drugs she doesn't really know about. She's quite interested – she'll ask, "What's it do? What's it like?" No, I remember having to go outside the studio to have a cigarette. Which is quite fair – she's paying the bill – it's her bloody record.'

He remembered Joan meeting Kate Bush once: 'Really funny, because Kate was really, "Oh, it's great to meet you!" And Joan really snubbed her!' And he laughs. They both like each other's music, 'but Joan came across as being really snotty. And she's *not*! And it was almost like me apologizing to Kate, saying, "Well, you know, Joan is...." It was quite funny.'

He agreed that Joan doesn't generally reveal much in interviews. 'She wouldn't tell you as much as the work would – and maybe other people.'

The Key is an album that radiates confidence right from the opening attack. Whether deliberately or not, this album has a very commercial feel about it – and not only the two tracks written at A&M's request for more commercial material. Here there are not only choruses – uncommon in Joan's writing – but many repeated lines, which confirm the assertive tone of this album.

'I wrote "Call Me Names" about two chaps in a band who were always arguing. They weren't poufs or anything but they were always at each other's throats.' (*Q* magazine September 1988.) Joan sings, 'It's their way of loving not mine', but cheerfully enters into the spirit of things, and Adrian Belew's distinctive solo perfectly fits the manic mood.

'Foolish Pride' is very poised, like Bryan Ferry, with tasteful brass. Joan's message is positive – 'Forget my pride ... Forget your foolish pride'. The mood of this album is very upbeat. On *Walk Under Ladders* Joan was using her confidence to take risks and throw challenges, but she takes the process even further here. The challenges on this album are all positive ones: Forget your pride – Drop the pilot – I've done it myself – Everybody gotta know this feeling – Give me the key to your heart! On 'The Key' she sings, 'They say that love is blind – and I'm blind I'm blind/ I know I'm blind' – she is revelling in her recklessness.

'Everybody Gotta Know' is less upbeat, but the message remains positive. Making mistakes, breaking habits, growing up, all these things can be difficult – but ultimately you have to to get anywhere: 'I've been there and it works.' In her early days with Pam Nestor, Joan was like a mother or big sister – disapproving. But now she is a very different big sister, giving the best kind of support. There are no 'victim' songs here. The two cover photos on the album are smiling - Joan is winning through – but on the inner sleeve she looks straight into the camera, serious, the most direct look we have ever seen from her.

Side two is big sister being street-wise and teasing a little – 'Tell Tale', which is delightfully ambiguous, and the sardonic 'What Do Boys Dream' and 'The Game Of Love'. But the synth solo on 'Game Of Love' is deep and dark, and 'The Dealer' is truly sinister, the harsh backing highlighting her accusing voice. But the mood is dropped suddenly and Joan is taunting us about 'Bad Habits' with Stones-style rock and Mel Collins delivering a punky sax solo. 'I Love My Baby' is a strange love song with its cold-blooded synthesizers sounding more like a walk in space than a cosy cuddle, a strange way to end this album.

Joan draws on various musical styles – Stax-style brass on 'Tell Tale', rhythm-and-blues and punk on 'Bad Habits' – but the clearest echoes throughout the album are the angular sounds of Bowie's *Scary Monsters* – not least Adrian Belew's guitar, which helped Bowie towards that seminal sound of the eighties. This influence would not have come only from Joan – Steve Lillywhite had worked with Bowie-philes Ultravox, and he must have kept his ears open too. And how many musicians were uninfluenced? The nasal backing vocals singing 'game of love' are an amusing reminder of Bowie's cockney delivery.

In February 1983 'Drop The Pilot' was released, producing Joan's second biggest hit ever at number eleven ('Love And Affection' went to number ten). While she does not take much account of singles hits, they can certainly help the sale of albums – though it should be noted that Joan's last two albums, *Me Myself I* and *Walk Under Ladders* went to numbers five and six without the real assistance of any single. Anyway, when *The Key* came out in March it went to number ten which was still respectable.

Before the end of the month Joan had begun another massive world tour which took her from Belfast to mainland Britain, Europe, then in June to the States and later Canada, Australia and New Zealand. This time Joan was having another complete turnaround, with a pretty young, all-British band, none of whom had played on the last album. She did cast back through her career for a couple of them – Julian Diggle from The Movies and Phil Palmer, the young guitarist who had played on *To The Limit*.

The other members were Mike Simmonds, keyboards and wind-synth, and Justin Hildreth on drums, who had played with two of Joan's studio keyboard players, Nick Plytas and Thomas Dolby. When the video *Track Record* came out in November to accompany the *Best of Joan Armatrading* album this was the band featured on many of the live tracks.

As with most of the tours, this one was long and exhausting, and people were complaining by the time they reached America. Joan has never broken through in the States to the extent she has elsewhere.

'For one thing I'm not American and for another I'm black. Over here if you're black you sing soul or reggae and it throws people that my songs aren't soul and aren't easily hummable. They don't expect me to speak like this – to them, to be black and English is weird.' The American market is strongly controlled by stereotypes. Even Michael Jackson was not played on MTV until his *fourth* number one hit, 'Billie Jean'.

The American tour was primarily a promotional exercise, and costs were kept to a minimum. The musicians, talented as they were, were relatively unknown and inexpensive, and the forty-man outfit travelled by road, the gear going by truck and the band and road crew on a coach. Even Joan travelled this way unless she was flying ahead for a special interview. Consequently the schedule was heavy, most gigs being followed by a long coach trip, often on the night of the gig. It was a hard slog covering the country and the venues varied considerably in size and prestige.

The man controlling the purse strings now was Mike Noble – the man who had first spotted Joan's potential on her demo tapes at Essex Music twelve years ago. When Joan made the move to A&M, he had followed, joining the A&R department. As Joan had become increasingly disenchanted with Mike Stone, her American manager, so Mike Noble had moved into this role. Although Joan was still signed to Mike Stone, a High Court battle would end that relationship the following year (1984). Joan is not particularly close to Mike Noble personally – which may be no bad thing in business.

'They have a strict, very businesslike, working relationship,' Phil Palmer explains. 'They don't go out to dinner or anything like that. Mind you,' he adds, 'Joan doesn't go out to dinner with anyone!'

'It's hard touring by coach, you know. You're exhausted when you get to places. We'd been doing this for three or four months, and I guess by that time people were complaining about how much driving there was to be done – especially the road crew because they sleep on the bus.'

Generally Mike Noble operated from his London office, but he did come out and join the tour in America.

'He started firing road crew, saying, "I don't want to listen to you complaining." He didn't realize what they have to go through to get the show going every night. Road crew are a strange breed.

'It was a comfortable bus, air-conditioned, television, all the rest of it, settees, but even so, it's horrible. Not only is it a long time on a bus, it's a long time to be cooped up with six other people. You just run out of things to say. So you end up trying to read a book, which is difficult on a bus, because you're bumping up and down, whatever. There were some hellish drives. I chose not to do that again.'

While Mike was with them he was given a nickname. 'At the time we were into crosswords and he became known as Emile Knob, which is an anagram of Mike Noble!' While the musicians did their crossword puzzles, Joan 'used to read *Beanos* a lot! And listen to her Walkman while staring out the window.

'It also makes it difficult with Joan being on the bus, because obviously she has a say in what you do, *if* you stop. She's always been a bit of a stickler about having anybody else on the bus who's not part of the band. So if your wife turns up to see a couple of shows, you have to rent a car – you can't ride on the bus. Things like that. She's just very protective about her space. She doesn't want anybody there.'

On stage the music was great. Joan played acoustic, but dabbled also with electric guitar. She is a tremendous musician, but one problem the band found was that they played the same set every night. 'Obviously there would be sound changes within the halls, [but] it was exactly the same, as far as possible,' says Phil. 'She was a bit of a stickler for that.

'I started out the tour thinking, OK, I'm gonna make a conscious effort to try and play something different every night. Just to keep yourself sane. But after six or seven weeks you run out of things to try. At the time I remember thinking, God, this is tedious.'

He looked forward to the encore. 'There was "Willow", which was always one of my faves. That was one of the only points in the set where things were likely to change. Not the structure but the feel. Depending what she was getting back from the audience, the song could stretch ... or contract – go very, very quiet ... quite loud. It was always flexible, but probably the only song in the set that was.'

He was never aware of Joan preparing or 'psyching herself up' for the performance. 'She's just how she is, and she doesn't change for anybody or anything. It really depends on the mood – some nights she'd be outgoing, communicate with the audience, other nights she wouldn't say a word.'

With such a busy schedule they didn't have much time for social life. But in Sydney, Australia, they went to the popular Manzil Room, a smart rock club. 'Joan got very keen on an all-girl Australian band, and we used to go and see them. She was talking about hiring them as her next touring band. It didn't come together. But they were good – good drummer especially.

'There were end-of-tour parties, and Joan would show up and smile at everybody and go away. Which is fine – that's how she is.'

Phil thinks he's the only musician to have kissed Joan: it was his birthday and on the spur of the moment he gave her a kiss right there on stage, which she didn't seem to mind.

'Joan is very ordinary in a lot of ways. People either think of her as a bit crazy, which I suppose maybe she is, or she's just this recluse – which I suppose she is as well! After six months on the road with her

I still didn't know her. And that is the only way to really get to know anybody – to work and live with them for six months, and travel and spend all your waking hours doing it. If you don't know someone at the end of that time ... she's deliberately putting up barriers.'

THIRTEEN

I write it down in invisible ink

Monday, 19 September 1983 was Independence Day for St Christopher (St Kitts) and Nevis. When her world tour ended in Australia, Joan flew to Antigua, and from there to Golden Rock airport, St Kitts, on the 16th. Stepping onto the hot tarmac in dark glasses and swinging a shoulder bag, she was met by an official reception committee and a local steel band. All this was filmed for the *Track Record* video which featured Joan's 'hits' and a couple of new songs.

We see Joan walking the dusty streets and even visiting the house where she was born – 'Is this where the Billinghursts used to live?' – climbing the steps to the verandah and being led through the rooms by a child even more taciturn than the teenage Joan. Joan herself appears unusually light-hearted and unselfconscious, glowing in the Caribbean sun. In contrast, Paul Gambaccini, accompanying her on this nostalgic trip, appears to be wilting. He has become Joan's 'official' interviewer in recent years, and asked her if she could feel that she came from here.

'I understand that I came from here, yes. I've always been curious ... never ... to the point of rushing to history books or asking my parents lots and lots of questions about the island or trying to conjure up my whole roots and stuff like that. But I've always wanted to see the place where I was born.... It's been a really strange experience, just walking round trying to visualize ...

'I have no memories of the island at all. Like my mum will tell me of being with my grandmother and running down the street. They do shaved ice here and they call it "freca" and she tells of me running down the street shouting for the guy that does the shaved ice, and stuff like that which I really wish I could remember.'

Joan was naturally interested in the music. She loved what she heard, 'but I don't know if it's this island's music. I think it's more Jamaican music – they've been playing lots of reggae and it's that dubbed reggae. They've played calypso music – that was really interesting – but it's the sort of calypso I heard in Antigua so I don't really know whether it's the music of all the islands or if they all had their own identity.'

Joan liked the mood of the place. 'Lots of innocence. They have a lot of morals that I find very confusing – they like to mess about! But even so they have this innocence still, where you can walk the streets at night and you can go up and talk to anybody.'

She was struck by the contrast that people in England have more money and live in nicer houses, but on the island there's friendliness and trust. 'The guys that don't work get looked after by their families or their friends. . . . In England, you don't work, you go to the dole, or if you're really down and out, you're down and out and you're on the streets and nobody would say Hullo to you.'

Joan played her guitar and sang at Warner Park for the Independence Day celebrations. She chose to play solo rather than bring her band along, although they had only just finished touring together.

The *Track Record* video came out in November. The songs and performances range from 'Steppin' Out' in 1973 to 'I'm Lucky' ten years later. Videos had never been Joan's strong point, and the early numbers are mimed with the contemporary bands, then 'Drop The Pilot' is the Godley and Creme video, which is well constructed, if largely irrelevant to the meaning of the song. The final section is excerpts from the 1983 show at Sydney – 'Rosie', 'I'm Lucky', a poised but vital 'Love And Affection', slightly hoarse but soulful 'Me Myself I' and 'Show Some Emotion', and the encore 'Willow', plus a couple of new songs, 'Frustration' and 'Heaven'. The 'tracks' are interspersed with interviews, and we see Joan 'at work' songwriting in her Boston hotel room with white Fender guitar and desk-top recorder. The package makes interesting if not compulsive viewing.

'"When I Get It Right", that was my first decent video, and that was Godley and Creme – they did a great job. I think they are great because in spite of me the video was good. But before I did the videos, because I was so self-conscious they didn't used to be very interesting, but now that I'm much more confident and into doing videos and being on stage, they come across a lot better, so now I can look at them and keep my eyes open! So "When I Get It Right" was really good; and then they did "The Weakness In Me" – that was good; and then the "Drop The Pilot" video was great, "What Do Boys Dream" was great; so there I am getting better all the time, which is good.'

'When I Get It Right', 'The Weakness In Me' and 'What Do Boys Dream' are extraordinary omissions from the video collection – especially as the first two are included on the album and CD. Maybe they weren't made in time.

In May 1984 Joan did an interview with Janice Long on Radio One. She said how she liked watching *Coronation Street* and *The World At War* on television, and films like *Trading Places*, *Superman* and *Airplane* ...

She said she used to write when she was on the road, but now has a room at home fitted up as an eight-track demo recording studio, and usually works in there from eleven o'clock in the morning until about eight or nine.

Of her recorded work she said, 'I always think that the songs are really good. I always think, that's a pretty good song there, Joan! Now and again I'll write something and I'll think, did I write that? Never mind!'

Four months later Joan was in the High Court. She was suing her former manager Mike Stone over the 1976 five-year management agreement which assured him commission on her earnings even after the agreement ended. Joan claimed the contract was invalid, sought details of money he had received on her behalf, and also sought damages. Mike Stone counter-claimed that Joan owed him money, and sought details of her earnings.

Two weeks later Mr Justice Leggatt declared that the contract, which had been 'loaded' by her manager to 'feather his own nest', was void. He said that when Miss Armatrading signed the agreement she did not understand it. She trusted Stone at that time, not knowing she would become a star. Stone must have known she was going to make it with her new album and, with their first contract nearing its end, had taken advantage of her trust to procure one which 'was in all respects beneficial to him'.

Nearly six weeks later Joan dropped her claim for damages, realizing that Stone had no money, and he in turn dropped his counter-claim. In due course Mike Stone returned to California to sell real estate.

With that unpleasant episode behind her, Joan turned her attention to the next album, *Secret Secrets*. This time her producer was Mike Howlett, who had worked with Martha and the Muffins (*Echo Beach*), OMD, Blancmange ('Living On The Ceiling'), China Crisis and Berlin. Joan had been going to record with Alex Sadkin (Grace Jones's producer), but for some reason he wasn't available at the last minute so Mike Howlett's manager called him up and said, 'How would you like to work with Joan Armatrading?' He 'leapt at it'.

'It was obvious on my first meeting with her she was very guarded, but in a friendly way – it's funny, she's got a knack of keeping people at a distance, but being friendly and relaxed at the same time.'

Joan had made complete demo tapes of all the songs and she played them to him. 'She'd done them all on an eight-track, full arrangements with drum-machines, guitar and all sorts of stuff – keyboards and things.'

Joan had recently moved, buying a beautiful farmhouse right out in the country to the west of London and starting to establish a studio in one of the old stone barns. Mike got to know Joan's studio very well – because Joan would not allow him to take any of the tapes away with him! 'So I had to go and sit with her and listen to the stuff' which was rather a problem.

'A lot of what I do is in the pre-production stage, in the arrangement stage, which I regard as very important. She had definite, arrangements, although a lot of the sounds were just basic. She was learning how to operate a desk at the time, which masked a lot of what was there.

'So I would go down and spend a day at a time with her, taking notes and mapping out charts of the songs, and *learning* the songs. Sometimes she'd leave me down there to listen to the stuff so I could work it all out.

'Once I'd got an idea what the songs were and had a few ideas about things, then we would go through and discuss where this happens, and where that chorus is too long, and so forth.'

Then they discussed musicians. Mel Gaynor (Simple Minds) on drums, was Joan's first choice as Steve Lillywhite had suggested him for *Walk Under Ladders*, but he hadn't been free.

'Joan has a thing about working with people too often. So I found myself in the position where I'd throw all these names at her, and you'd go, "Phil Palmer's a good guitarist."

' "Oh no, no, he played on my third album...."

' "What about...?"

' "I think he did a tour with me in 1979...."

'She'd say it wasn't anything wrong with them at all but just that she liked to work with somebody new. I know she worked with Jerry Marotta twice, and he said he was surprised that she let him work with her again!

'What was really nice with her – and strange too – was that when I said, "Pino Palladino," I don't think she knew who he was, but she liked the sound of his name. Then "David Rhodes", a friend of mine, and she said, "Oh – oh yes, why, who's he play with?" Now she'd never heard of him but she really liked the sound of his name, and then I'd fill her in on who he was.

'And the same with studios too. We went to look at a lot of places before we booked anything, and just as soon as we'd walk in the door she'd go, *"Nooo...."* I wouldn't have booked anything without ... because she was like that and I think it's very important. Joan was obviously the kind of person who you absolutely had to steer very gently as she really knows what she wants – even when she doesn't know what it is yet!'

Joan finally chose Battery Studios in Willesden, which was a pleasant if embarrassing surprise for Mike as it was owned by the people who manage him. But Joan knew the studio when it was Morgan, from the double-bass sessions on *Back To The Night*.

'She remembered it as soon as she walked in the door, and she said, "Oh yes, yes!" So I ended up in the studio I basically wanted to be at anyway. For me that sums up a lot of things about her, which I think is great. It's not rational, but it works. A very accurate way of going about things.'

They were working late sessions, which posed the problem of where to eat. Mike suggested Rebecca, a cook he knew from working at the

Manor. 'So we would have a sit-down dinner at about seven o'clock – on the snooker table! When we had all the band in there it was quite fun.' Rebecca was credited on the album.

Once the band was assembled, recording went ahead pretty smoothly. 'I like to prepare things, with those guys here. Firstly they were too expensive to mess around – well, we had them all on basic – two weeks lump sum, basically. David Rhodes stayed on for three weeks – to re-shoot. It all worked well.

'Whenever I do a live band I always try to separate out everything as much as possible.' At Battery One Studio there is the main large room, then a smaller room off it which is completely soundproofed, where Mike put all the guitar amps, as he had first tried with Flock of Seagulls.

David Rhodes (guitar) had his amp in the back room but played in the control room. Pino Palladino and Nick Pleytas (bass and keyboards) were also in the control room, plugged in direct. Mel's drums were set up in the main studio of course, and Joan also played out there behind a screen. Mel is a very loud, powerful drummer, and they went for his big kit sound, using the natural ambience of the studio.

Mike remembers reading an interview with Joan, 'saying how I got her to use different snare drums on different songs – which I did – and how she felt that was quite an interesting idea. Which is against the grain of modern American production style where you get *a sound* for the whole record.

'There's a good story which I think is very much Joan's way of working. We were knocking out the backing tracks – track-a-day sort of thing. We ran through a song and all the guys went back in the control room listening back to a take. Then Joan said to Mel, about the drumming, "You know, Mel, in the middle-eight you do this bit – *do-ba-do-ba-DOO, da-DA, ba-da-DOO* – you know what it's like?"

' "Yeah, yeah!"

'She said, "Well, don't."

'And that was it! I don't know how she did it – it wasn't a put-down. . . . I found that remarkable.'

Joan played acoustic guitar on the basic tracks. She also played electric parts on the overdubs, but decided against using them. 'There were some electric things which I thought she did really well,' Mike says, 'but she'd rather have the hired-gun do it because he'd do it better and she didn't feel that her guitar playing was up to it. But I thought it was. We might have ended up getting her to do a bit under duress.'

Both Mike and Joan thought strings would be a good idea on 'Persona Grata'. He saw it as similar to 'Love And Affection'. They discussed arrangers and somebody suggested Fiachra Trench. Mike had not worked with him before, but he seemed good-natured – fortunately, as it turned out.

The three of them would discuss, then Joan and Fiachra would work together at a keyboard. So it came to the day when there was a fifteen-piece string section in the big studio with Fiachra conducting.

'They did a run through with the tape, and I think about half-way through the second run through Joan said, "No, no – no. It's got to stop."

'So I had to walk out in the middle of it all, and go, "Stop everyone!" Stop them all and say, "I think you should come inside and have a talk."

'Fiachra said, "A couple of points?"

' "I think it's a bit more serious than that!"

'So while the whole orchestra's sitting there – we're paying them thousands of pounds, God knows what – Fiachra came back in, and we actually sat and went through the whole thing in the control room, Joan going, "No, this – out! This – out. Not there – out!" And it was such a sight! Great red crosses through the whole thing! And – why not? It was nerve-racking for me – I'd very rarely worked with string sections. They're a pretty uncooperative bunch, but Joan has enormous respect from musicians of all kinds.'

Mike Howlett believes that vocals are so important that he uses a good mike even for guide vocals early on. 'For me, it's the single most important thing on any record – especially with a singer-songwriter. But I'd heard that Bryan Ferry was very shy about being seen singing in the studio, and that he used to build a kind of house for himself out of screens, covered with blankets. I suggested this to Joan and she thought it was a great idea. So we built a house – it was wonderful! Quite an intricate thing with a passageway to get to the centre.'

One song where this 'hide' could not be used was 'Love By You', a beautiful duet, where Joan was simply accompanied on piano by Joe Jackson, another A&M artist.

'I love that,' says Mike, 'because I'd say ninety per cent of that was just one take. We really did it, piano and voice at the same time, and then we just patched up a few vocal lines. It's very particular.

'I think that they had eye-contact – from a distance. I don't know, it was dark! I have a picture in my mind of Joan sitting on a stool, looking at him. But it seems almost wrong – too "cabaret"! It may have been the picture we were trying to create, and the reality was she was in a bunker somewhere! It was great with her and Joe – once he relaxed a bit. Because Joe again is a very guarded, cautious person, but very pleasant, well-mannered, nice – I don't know the word. That was really quite interesting to see because it was a bit like . . . hedgehogs negotiating!'

It was Joe who suggested the brass section – they had just worked on a big swing album with him. The quartet – two trumpets and trombone, led by Dave Bitteli on sax – were working with Wham at the time, and had recorded with the flugelhorn and trumpet player, Raul D'Oliviera, who also played lead on 'Talking To The Wall'. Mike is a big fan of flugelhorn as he used to play in brass bands. Dave worked on the brass arrangements with Joan, which was a similar process to the string arrangements, except that there were fewer instruments to deal with so Dave could be more flexible.

This was the last album on which Joan worked with a producer. She had always been very sure about her musical ideas and throughout her recording career she had been slowly acquiring the expertise needed to realize these ideas on tape. There is often an ambivalence in the relationship of artist and producer as their respective talents come into play. Joan herself, while occasionally denying that she wanted to produce herself, nonetheless expressed her reservations about the contribution of a producer. By the time she came to work with Mike Howlett she was so confident in the studio that she obviously regarded him as little more than an aid to recording – a glorified engineer. Naturally Mike felt this was unsatisfactory.

'Joan was good to work with, but I felt at the end of the whole project a *little* bit frustrated. I actually said to her at a certain point, "Really you should think about doing it yourself because you really need a good engineer – somebody to pull the pieces together, and that's probably the way you'll be happiest." I find it interesting that she has since decided, after working with me, never to work with a producer again!'

'I made the decision,' says Joan, 'while I was making the last album. I felt that I'd got to the stage where I could do it on my own. I was quite happy working with the other producers – I was relying on them for sound. It also helped me to work with different people so I could learn more about sound and how to communicate with engineers better.'

The only area in which Mike felt Joan had really needed him was in recording vocals – always a difficult process to do oneself.

'There I would really be doing my job, and I'd really push her in places, and say, "Go for that again." And then I'd do a detailed breakdown and composite vocal – the usual thing. She would leave me to it, but then come in and then we'd get into real nitty gritty stuff. And she would be great – very picky – about whether that note was really perfectly in tune, and so forth. As usual, sometimes too far. With singers, sometimes it's not whether it's in tune or not that's important – it's whether you've the right vibe for that. I did as well as I could. It's not a bad album. But I said it to her at the time, that really she should be going much more acoustic again. I wanted her to head much more back towards "Love And Affection", which was my favourite stuff. Although I'm known as a synthi/electro producer, that's not why she used electronics *at all*. It's entirely what she was doing. But nevertheless, I love what she does.'

At the time they were recording *Secret Secrets* Mike's wife was pregnant, and Joan took such an interest that they went and visited her with the baby afterwards. 'She was very keen to see him, and he threw up all over her! Also when we were in Atlanta, in '85 I did an album in Atlanta, and she came to town and I saw her show and arranged to see her at the hotel afterwards, and she asked, "Can you bring Toby in?" So we sat in the hotel lobby while she played with Toby – had a chat. That might be the last time I saw her though.'

On the cover of *Secret Secrets* we see Joan Armatrading in a dress for the first time, though it's a rather coat-like dress. In her right hand she holds a pair of flat-heeled shoes, in her left a piece of burning paper. The reddish glow on her face suggests she may have just started a fire – or is it a letter she's burning? Robert Maplethorpe's photo takes her in from lips to knees, but cuts off the upper part of her face. On the back cover Joan covers her mouth, hiding a smile, perhaps, and on the inner sleeve she covers her ears, this time grinning broadly. 'See no evil ...'?

Secret Secrets starts big, with some of the swagger of *The Key*, but 'Persona Grata' is more orchestral, like some of the rock epics of the seventies. It is also more ominous, and the messages on this album are very different. Now we are given a glimpse of the fears which lie behind the brashness and confidence.

The first three songs are about being in someone's power, and the whole album is about failed or problematic relationships. 'Temptation' is about fear of love, but not simply paranoia – 'Takes you where/ You want to be' – this is also the excitement of danger, that *frisson* before stepping on stage, and Joan's voice gives a new lift to 'Lead me not into/ Temptation' which every Christian-taught schoolkid has muttered in assembly. 'Moves' seems to hark back to the crippling shyness of Joan's earlier years – which presumably has not entirely left her. The music is 'up', but some of this may be the energy of frustration – 'Rooted to the/ Stupid floor'. We are treated to a rare burst of echoy, sixties blues harmonica from Joan here.

'Talking To The Wall' has Joan moving into cool jazz territory – the first hint of the next album. The flugelhorn stating the theme is a nice image of Joan's own voice – mellow, with pure high notes. 'I wanted to create something romantic,' she says, 'something you can close your eyes to and just listen.' The two voices weave together producing strange harmonies which are a feature of this album – maybe Joan's keyboards have led her here. Joan's paradox of the 'friendly wall' may be a reflection of herself – or at least the persona she presents to the world – solid, listening, but producing a stony silence. Joan likes walls for their strength, security and privacy.

The plain piano on 'Love By You' is reminiscent of Joan's early style, but played with Joe's sensitivity and sureness of touch. 'I seem to always like to have something calm at the end of each record side. The same at concerts. You must have something to calm you down a bit.'

On side two we are swimming in synths and Joan seems to have gone overboard on wild intros, although on the first two tracks these merely lead into fairly regular songs. Only 'Persona Grata' is big enough to take this treatment. 'One Night' has Joan in very fine voice, but might have been more effective with a less relentless backing. The title track has Joan dabbling in punk – very adeptly, though it's taken at breakneck 'live' tempo. Needless to say, perhaps, this is one song Joan happily admits is about her!

Then, in contrast, 'Strange' has the magic of simplicity as Joan gives free reign to her talent for ballads. She captures the confusion and numbness that is left when love falls apart. Each side of this album begins with bombast and ends in a simple statement of loss.

Secret Secrets went to number fourteen in the British charts, seventy-three in the States, and produced no hit singles. While it was being recorded Joan was auditioning people for the next world tour. One of the first musicians to be chosen was Steve Greetham.

Steve was playing bass for Annabel Lamb, who was signed to A&M Records and managed by Mike Noble. They had just finished an album and there wasn't much happening. So Annabel mentioned these auditions and Mike said, 'Yeah, go up for it,' and Steve did three auditions. The first one was at the Battery studios where Joan was just finishing off the album.

'I went there and she played a backing track off *Secret Secrets*. There wasn't any bass on it, just chord patterns and bits. Joan gave me a chord sheet and said, "Here you are – have a go at that." It was something that most people could play, and I think maybe she wanted to hear just how you actually played it – and how you related to her telling you what to do, I think, more than anything.

'Then there was a band audition at Nomis and they were obviously auditioning a few other people – drummers and that. I thought, well, I'll probably be one of the bass guitarists here, and I turned up and said, "I haven't brought any equipment with me, I assumed you'd hired a stack."

'And they said, "No, but we will."

'I said, "Haven't you got anybody else coming?"

'She said, "No."

'I thought, does that mean I've got the job?

'It was like, you were always left wondering, oh, is *that* what she meant?

'There was Les Davison on guitar, Alex White on keyboards, Jim Ross on saxophones, vocals and guitar. And Ted Emmett on trumpet,

Mark Parnell on drums. So it was quite a large line-up, but we all did vocals and stuff and Jim and Ted did the dancing.

'We played everywhere – we did three months in the States, a month in Europe, three weeks over here, three weeks in Australia, and we did one show in Tel Aviv, a live open-air concert.

'She was a great performer – that was the thing that amazed me, not having seen her before. Doing a month's rehearsal – big deal, you rehearse, that's all you do, you learn the songs. And once she actually got out she was brilliant and I was absolutely stunned.

'For months I was stunned because I couldn't believe this woman, this introspective, tender woman, could perform like that. She was like a real rock-'n'-roll star, running round on the top of the PA tower and occasionally using the hall. There was one hall with a little royal box in the middle, and she got the roadies to guard her running down with a radio mike – the audience didn't know where she was. It was real fun! I was amazed that she was like that.'

The two-hour show mixed about seven numbers from *Secret Secrets* with the usual selection of older numbers.

'Three encores every night – easily,' says Steve. 'Always ended in "Willow". I hated that number. I dunno why – I never really liked it that much. And because it was the last number of the night and it was slow, it always bugged me that we weren't going out on a big one. But reaction was incredible. Obviously she was doing it because it worked, and every night it worked.

'Towards the end of the tour she relaxed a lot more with people generally, so you could have a bit of a fool around. But there was a line over which you couldn't step – musically and socially. I remember she used to pick a member of the band every night to introduce the rest of the band. That was because at first she couldn't remember everybody's names.' They didn't usually introduce Joan herself, but: 'Somebody did that one night and got a real black look, well, I'd say an unpleasant look. But obviously three or four months into the tour you'd started fooling around a bit. Some nights you'd overstep the mark and Joan would give you a bit of a ragging afterwards, semi-serious. She'd tell you off, or say, "I don't know if that was a very good idea." But there was always this twinkle in her eye, because she was almost being one of the boys without being one of the boys. She wanted to be one, but keep her distance.'

Inevitably Joan got closer to some musicians than others – 'I think because they were the naughtier ones. She quite enjoyed the fact that people weren't being as good as they could be.

'It was fun for about the first two months. Some of the shows were great – some of the shows I did with Joan were among the best shows I've ever done with anybody in my whole life. Like Tel Aviv and Red Rocks – those are really memorable. But once you get two-and-a-half months into a tour you start getting tour-blind. But she was a great trooper, because she'd been doing it forever. She always got the enthusiasm.'

Considering the toughness of the schedule Joan's voice held out very well. There was only one night, fairly early on in the tour, when she was in trouble.

'It was pretty bad but she managed to get through. Jim Ross doubled up for her on the high notes, because she could sing quite low and husky – her range was good, but she couldn't get all the way up one night. But in six months she hardly had much trouble at all.'

Joan did look after herself, of course, and backstage arrangements were very civilized. Joan had her own dressing room and the tour had its own caterer. 'Joan didn't eat that much of *anything* that I ever noticed – she was never a glutton. A few packets of M&Ms [chocolate] were consumed, if I remember rightly. She never drank – I never saw her drink any alcohol.'

As usual the American leg of the tour was the hardest. In New York they played a couple of nights at Radio City and also did a gig at the Ritz, which Steve describes as 'a thousand-seater shit-hole like the Marquee.

'I think they did it for fun more than anything else, because we couldn't take our own gear in. And it was like playing a grungy, rock-'n'-roll two hours on stage doing that. But that was fun too – well, it would have been if we hadn't had to get in the coach and drive twelve to fourteen hours and get out and do a matinée *and* another evening show. So inside of twenty-four hours we actually did three gigs.

'One thing I didn't quite get was why Joan was never really that popular in the States. Everywhere she went it was close to being sold out – two nights at Radio City sold out and nine-and-a-half thousand people at Red Rocks, but it was a bit patchy. It was having to do everywhere – Kalamazoo and places like that – "What are we doing there?"'

In America, as in Britain, the audiences were ninety per cent white.

'Americans are generally very ignorant because they're so far away from the rest of the world that they don't feel that they have to be informed of it. They didn't believe there were any black people in England. Some places we used to stop at a truck-stop and there was these guys in red-man hats and stetsons looking at her, "What the fuck's she doing here?" – with us. It looked like we got off the bus from Mars. Yeah, it was a bit peculiar, but it was fun.

'As a band we were hired hands, really, but you soon formed your attachments to people. It also got us a bit closer to Joan. We were her boys, but only to the extent that she wanted us to be. She'd take it so far and that was it.'

In June they finally flew to Australia, perhaps Joan's favourite country, and one where she is adored. The tour came to a glorious end in Sydney, where she was given the key to the city.

'We did six nights at Sydney Entertainment Centre. It wasn't a record, but I was pretty stunned. They really do love her out there.

'Quite a lot of people would like to get backstage and get autographs, as there always is, but I don't think it was anything great for her. She'd sign autographs but she didn't make a big deal of it. I think the actual being on stage seemed to be it for her, and afterwards that was the end of the show – time to go home.

'A few found the hotel and would hang around outside, but it was never a big thing at all. You get more of that kind of thing going on with male rock acts. With Joan it was much more a mature acceptance of what she did, and respect from her audience as well. We used to remark as a band that it was fairly boring from that point of view! You never used to get yourselves thrown at! I didn't come back with much swag! Just memories.'

During her quiet moments on the road Joan was often writing. She always has a guitar to hand, and in her hotel room she had a portable recording set-up. Towards the end of the tour she would occasionally try new ideas out with the band at sound checks.

'They were fairly amorphous at the time,' Steve reports. 'From doing the album after the tour I can't recognize any of the bits. She was just fooling around with things. But we really didn't have that much time.

It wasn't very serious on her behalf to get anybody involved in doing it at that stage.'

After the tour was officially over Joan did an extra open-air concert in Tel Aviv. In July there was the double Live Aid concert in Britain and America, but Joan did not appear, which was a surprising omission. Steve Greetham recalls that they were supposed to do Live Aid, but Bill Graham wanted her for America and Joan and the band were in Britain and somehow got left off the bill.

In November Joan started work on the next album. Steve wasn't expecting to be asked to do any studio recording. He was well aware that Joan's touring and recording bands tended to be of a different calibre: talented unknowns on the road and the big-name session guys in the studio. However, he was in for a surprise – this time Joan was going to need more continuity. She was steppin' out again.

FOURTEEN

Take it from me

'I've produced this album myself, but that's always been something I would eventually do – I've always been so involved with the records. I've only relied on the producer to help me get the sound. All the little bits in the music that you hear on my records that people would normally attribute to the producer, I do. By the time I finished *Secret Secrets* I'd made up my mind that the next album I would produce myself. Then, once I started to write and do the demos, I decided that home would be the best place to be totally relaxed. I've got the studio in my home and I've always done my demos at home, and I thought, well, it's all here, why don't I just make the record here?'

There was one very good reason why not. It would mean the expensive process of upgrading her studio, and Joan didn't want to make another album only to have it fail A&M's 'quality control'. So she decided to play it safe and do a trial run with a couple of members of the tour band, Steve Greetham and Alex White (bass and keyboards). They drafted in a drummer they knew, Geoff Dugmore, and Joan would play all the guitars.

'We thought it was weird that we'd been asked to do it,' says Steve, 'because our impression was that she always kept the touring band as working musicians, just journeymen really, and then the people that she had on her album were special – stars. But it was obviously a new thing that she was trying and we were very pleased to be able to do it.'

Joan had already made some demos of the songs with drum-machine, electric guitar and keyboard. She had sketched in some rudimentary bass lines on keyboard, guitar or even her own bass. On tour she had occasionally had a go on Steve's bass. 'She also liked drums. She would have a bit of a bash around on Parnell's kit. She wasn't very good, but she was all right – if she'd have kept it up she probably would have been able to do it.

'I do remember there being some specific bass lines she wanted me to play, but in playing them you tend to do other things as well, and she'd immediately pick up on that and incorporate it. Or she'd take all the elements she liked about what you were playing and put them together for you, which I did find quite interesting.

'We started in November, and in two or three weeks of going down for a few days at a time doing a couple of tracks, it seemed like it was gonna work there, and it was gonna work with *us*.'

'That was going so well,' says Joan, 'that in the middle of it I decided that the studio was working but the equipment wasn't good enough. So right in the middle of making *Sleight Of Hand* I decided to upgrade my studio, so I got a twenty-four track tape machine, drums and everything. All that was going on around me, and I feel as if I can hear some sort of tension on *Sleight Of Hand*, as if I'm not really relaxed.'

Mark Wallis was drafted in as engineer and in January 1986 the serious sessions started, still with the same basic band. Bumpkin Studios, as Joan had christened it, was now very attractive.

'It was old stables,' says Steve, 'but it had been done out really nicely. It was quite comfortable.' Upstairs was the control room, which was now the main recording room, in these days when amps were dispensed with and many instruments would be plugged direct into the desk. Downstairs the stables had been turned into a drum room with a very good 'live' sound – stone flagged floors and wood panelling. There were also storage bays and even a games room.

'I'd be in the control room,' says Steve. 'So would the keyboard player, and Joan and the drummer would be downstairs. Basically we learnt the number and played it through, and all we did it to was a click track, the drums, bass and keyboards. Joan played guitar, but she didn't actually play along with us. I think we worked it up between me, the drummer and the keyboard player, so we laid the tracks like that. So we did them, got the drum take, went back and I'd repair any bass, and the keyboards, then went on to do separate parts and then Joan would come in and do some guitar.

'Her acoustic is amazing – absolutely amazing. If she did do an album that was mainly [acoustic] and back to the old songs she'd probably sell a bucket-load. But she can't play electric guitar to save her life, though she'd hate anybody for saying that because she really tries, worked really hard.'

Perhaps aware of the critical attitude of her fellow musicians, Joan always cleared the studio when she was playing guitar.

'It was just her and the engineer. She was very specific about the working conditions. It was her own house and the privacy involved was possibly more than was necessary. We weren't allowed to wander around the grounds or go in any other part of the building at all.'

Once the basic tracks were recorded Joan called in a few more musicians for overdubs. Steve and Alex now realized why they had been chosen for this album.

'Joan had already worked with me and Alex for six months so she knew that we would be sympathetic. I know she had a guitarist in, that she'd never met, to do one track – Eddie Golga – and I don't think he had the easiest time of it. Because she didn't know him, it was a fairly cold thing. She's very cold when you meet her, and it takes a long time to break that down. And you get to a stage where you know you'll never go beyond. Very few people will ever go beyond that I think.'

After the basic tracks and the overdubs, Joan recorded guide vocals, also in seclusion, then the next stage was backing vocals. For once Joan was not singing these herself, which may have been because she was producing, or of course because she liked the sound they had achieved on tour. Steve was delighted.

'I did the rhythm tracks, then I went back to do the backing vocals at the end, so we got to hear it pretty much all the way through. It was really interesting. There was me, Geoff Dugmore and Jim Ross doing backing vocals together. She'd give us an idea of what she wanted, though I think on one occasion we came up with something different. She wanted us to sing really high, and Jim and Geoff could just about manage it, but I couldn't on one number.'

After that Joan sang her lead vocals in seclusion and the recording was complete.

'She got Steve Lillywhite in at the end to do the mix. He was only going to mix the single, but at the end of the day he mixed the whole album: which was good, because even though I felt she produced well – she got the best out of everybody and the best out of the situation – it's still like a different job to do mixing. It's best to say, "Here you are, this is how I want it to sound, go and mix it." So I think that worked really well.'

The album starts exuberantly with a *whoop!* and settles into a comfortable rock groove. Joan is producing herself at last and she sings her heart out. 'Kind words and a real good heart/ Doesn't mean you get respect' – the song could be casting an ironic eye back over her life – 'You gotta make your own beginning'! Steve Lillywhite's mix is clean and although synthesizers are well to the fore, the songs don't drown in them.

Joan gave a very full interview to *Tracks* magazine in which she explained the thoughts behind each song. 'There's a line in the song ["Kind Words"] "You can't always tell the bad guys cos they don't always dress in black," – you know, so you just have to watch yourself.

' "Killing Time" is somebody saying you can go out and have your fun, but I'll be here waiting when you come back because we've had some good times together.' That is what Joan says, but the lyric is much more bitter than that. 'I'm left killing time/ It's a homicide/ A ritual/ Don't treat a human like that.'

This song contains the album's title, *Sleight Of Hand*, and if this album has a theme it is cunning and deceit. As someone who wants a lot of trust, Joan is quick to suspect duplicity. Her wit does not desert her, however, for it is also a nice metaphor for the fact that she is (virtually) the only guitarist on the album. On the cover Snowdon pictures a cheerful Joan with a black Fender guitar. The angle is unusual, so we only see the back of the guitar, and in silhouette. On the back cover there is a striking study of Joan's fingers in action, red nail varnish matching the guitar. She is plucking a string on the neck, a very original technique, if genuine.

Apart from Eddie Golga's distant contribution on 'Laurel And The Rose', all the guitars are Joan, and all electric – there is no vestige here of the acoustic sound which first captured our ears. Joan's first solo here is a nice echoy Shadows sound, nothing too risky.

'Reach Out' (another Motown reference) has Joan slapping the effects on and sounding more like the seventies guitar hero while Wesley Magoogan's sax recalls Clarence Clemons. Just as *Walk Under Ladders* looked ahead to Adrian Belew's guitar on *The Key*, so here we can hear Joan heralding the approach of Mark Knopfler on *The Shouting Stage*. The lyric is decidedly banal, however, adding nothing to the message of 'Willow'.

The idea for 'Angelman' came from a film script Joan was sent. 'It was about a bloke who was a real bad lad, but he seemed to want everyone to think he was an angel. Also my brother at one point was in this series called *Angels* and he said to me that they called him Angel Man.' (Joan's younger brother, actor Tony Armatrading, now twenty-five, played the male nurse Josh Jones.)

This is another of Joan's tirades against men behaving as men do – when they can get away with it, and it confirms the album as an exercise in Heavy Metal – which is not to dismiss it, for it is a fine album, very tuneful. What it is not, of course, is what Joan's early albums led us to expect, but that is Joan's business – if she is content to sell moderately. 'Laurel And The Rose' is more poetic, a beautiful song, although here Joan's voice is a little swamped. She describes it as 'a love song which is saying, "I'm not sure how much you're to be trusted, but I'm going to take the chance that you're the right person and let's get married." '

'One More Chance' is a dramatic production with a full stagey voice, and overtones of Prince's influential 1999. This is the first album where Joan uses backing vocals – her band – to any great extent. The lyric is a return to the theme of 'Everybody Gotta Know'. 'Jesse' (also based on a film script) is more sleight of hand – 'You can do magic'.

'I like "Figure Of Speech" because it's quite empty and then you suddenly get the drums. The song is saying, "When this bloke says he loves you, it's really just a figure of speech – he doesn't really. He's after every woman in the world. But don't think this is the end of the world, there's going to be somebody else." '

'Don Juan' was Joan's favourite track – 'because I find it very romantic. It's just a nice, soppy love song, so I like that.' In it she states clearly her most constant appeal – 'I want that very special love.' Joan is different from most pop writers in that she is never simply 'looking for someone to love'. A love that is not special is just not worth having. This is a profound truth – how many people end up in unsatisfactory relationships because they are afraid of being alone? – but it also underlines Joan's problem of being extremely mistrustful – can *anyone* provide the exacting love she is seeking?

'I like to write the lyrics and have them mean something and be sensible, yet I'm much more at ease talking on a musical level, because the lyrics are there and you can see them. I take more notice of the sound of the record as well. There is one track that I didn't play the guitar on, "Laurel And The Rose", but I worked out the parts and I really enjoyed it. I played harmonica. I didn't play any keyboards, although I do on the demos – and when I'm writing I play all sorts of bits. If there's a little sax part that I want, then I'll play the sax, but the instrument I can really play is the guitar.

'What I do when I'm composing is first of all write the song on piano or guitar and then work out the arrangements. So I work out what the bass part should be, then I put that down on tape, then I work out the keyboard part and put that down and so on. I don't work out people's solos, but the actual parts. When the musicians arrive, they've got a complete song to listen to. All they've got to do is listen to what their instrument is and play that.'

Sleight Of Hand is not a particularly profound album, but still one Joan can be very proud of. In its strong rock style, it feels like a record she had wanted to make for a long time. As Joan told Paul Gambaccini in 1988, 'I was really pleased with *Sleight Of Hand* because I did all the guitar, and there's a lot of good guitar playing on it. But I wasn't totally pleased with all the songs. When I did them I thought, that's really good, but when I listen to a song like "Jesse" now I hate it! But there's a song on there called "One More Chance" which I think is brilliant – sorry, but it is!'

In April, waiting for the album to be released, Joan spoke at unusual length to the *Standard* about her life away from stage and studio.

'I live alone in my house in Surrey [near Guildford] where I've converted a room into a recording studio. Friends who visit me would describe my furnishings as sparse. I like to have minimal clutter. I have a large garden and I grow potatoes, leeks, peas and all the berries you can think of.

'I like to watch horror films on television by myself. Then I'm scared to go to bed in case The Thing comes through the floorboards. I listen to whatever is on the radio, but when I'm writing or recording, I don't listen to anything else. I liked Kate Bush's LP *Hounds Of Love*.

'I love driving. I have a 1938 Austin Seven and a black and cream convertible Vauxhall, which looks like a Noddy car. I'm a good driver, although I wrote off my Honda last year. I was driving along the A3 when I put my brakes on and the car went out of control. I veered off the road and knocked down a couple of trees. I was very lucky. The other car I hit belonged to an off-duty policeman.

'I'm a vegetarian, but I eat fish. My favourite restaurant is a fish and chip shop behind the Gate Cinema in Notting Hill. I like to sit there and compare people with the fish they're eating. I don't know what they think of me! I don't drink alcohol or tea or coffee. Mostly I drink water. I've never smoked.

'I don't enjoy shopping. I like track suits and T-shirts and I do wear frocks sometimes. I've just bought a silky one in Sloane Square. It's the most expensive thing I've ever bought – about £200.

'I don't go to parties. I don't really know what to say to people – I'm shy.'

Sleight Of Hand came out in May and did moderately well. The single, 'Kind Words (And A Real Good Heart)' failed to chart. It was time for another of those notorious world tours. Geoff Dugmore and Steve Greetham decided against going. Geoff was working and Steve couldn't face another six months on the road.

'I think she felt let down because she'd let us into doing her album. She felt it was not a particularly nice way of being. So we didn't part on great terms. I was always sad about it – it was taken the wrong way.'

Six months later the pressure proved too much even for Joan.

'At the end of that tour,' she said, 'having done that after so many records, I was incredibly tired – too tired to stand up. I came off the stage and just fell down and had to be carried off into the dressing room. I felt really sorry for them cos they were carrying this lump, poor things! I'd had enough – I was just too tired. So I couldn't finish the whole tour.'

'They ended up blowing out quite a lot of the tour,' says Steve, 'like Australia and some of America. Alex White, Les Davison and Jim Ross went on to do the tour, and we kept in touch. They said this one's not quite as good, and she's not quite as good. I got the impression she'd hit a bit of a low point in sales and in her career and although the albums she was bringing out and the music she was making was good, I don't think the public wanted to hear it – they wanted to hear what she used to do more than anything else.'

None of the musicians want to talk about that period, but Phil Palmer also heard a rumour that she wasn't completely happy with the band.

'I don't know the exact reasons, but I think she took it upon herself to make it work – she just took on too much.'

Joan took a year off. 'For most of that time I didn't have anything to do with music. I just slept, drove around a bit, sat in the garden, watched a bit of television, but didn't play my guitar, I didn't write, didn't listen to much music or anything.'

Joan made a conscious decision not to work so intensively. She would take her time over the next album and there would be no more six-month world tours. This formula worked, and she later said, 'The last tour was about two months – that's the shortest I've ever done. It was nice! And I thought, I've made so many albums and I seem to have been here for a little while, maybe I don't need to keep pushing myself as hard as I do.'

FIFTEEN

All a woman needs

The Shouting Stage was a wonderful experience for all involved. Joan was happy and relaxed, working at home in a comfortable, modern studio, and was giving herself all the time in the world. She usually took six weeks to record an album, but this time she began in September 1987 and finished the following May.

'What I did was I wrote, and listened to that, then I recorded, then I re-recorded.' Joan also had far more freedom in her choice of musicians. 'If somebody said, "Well, I'd love to do it but I can only do it in two months' time," then there was no panic – I had the two months' time.'

Some of these musicians were top-flight session men, and some had worked with Joan before, but years ago – drummers Jamie Lane from The Movies in 1975, and Dave Mattacks from *Joan Armatrading* days, and guitarist Phil Palmer who had toured with Joan in 1983 and last recorded with her on *To The Limit*. As Jamie puts it, 'Joan always changes musicians and the circle had come round again.'

Phil says, 'Joan doesn't really have a social life, but when we are working, especially down at her house, it's a good atmosphere, friendly, relaxed. I think she always felt under pressure in big London studios, because obviously it's very expensive and she has no time to experiment. So I think it's the best thing she ever did, to build her own studio.'

This time Graham Dickson was the engineer, recommended by Gus Dudgeon.

'Graham's done a lot of work with Elton John,' says Jamie. 'He just takes care of all that angle. You can hear basically how she wants it done by the demo, but the specifics one tends to do by trial and error. It's not so much a case of Joan saying, "Do it like this, do it like that." If she doesn't like a sound he'll work until she likes it.'

'Nice equipment, everything works,' says Phil. 'It's very clean – you're not allowed to smoke or drink tea in the control room! You have to go out of the studio if you want to do anything like that. I suppose it's quite quaint really – another one of Joan's little things. She just drinks boiled water. And eats chocolate – there's always a big bowl of Mars Bars, Milky Ways, all that stuff.'

'There's always great food laid on,' Jamie confirms. 'When you get there, there's coffee, a loaf of bread and some cheese, a bowl of fruit. It's always pretty civilized, we turn up at eleven, ease into it gently, break the ice, she'll go down and make a cup of tea for everybody and find some biscuits, make sure everyone's looked after. And then in the evening there is dinner, then back for another couple of hours or so, and then break for the next day.' The studio is within reach of London so no one stays overnight.

'The latest I've ever been there is about ten o'clock when we just had to get something finished. But the pace of work is very relaxed. There's never any sort of *Angst*. That's the advantage of having your own studio. When I was doing some of the new album the good weather had already started....'

'It's a lovely house,' says Phil – 'beautiful part of the country. She has this courtyard affair, with a stone drive – chips. Then we all drive our cars in there and the gates are closed behind us, and we're cut off from the rest of the world. One afternoon whilst we were having a break, she got a broom out and she was going around getting rid of the tyre marks from the gravel!'

Dave Mattacks remembers, 'I was just having a stroll around the grounds and she leaned out the window and said, "I'd rather you didn't go over there." '

Later when he went to dinner at Gus Dudgeon's with Mike Noble, Dave commented, 'Joan hasn't changed much about the privacy. I couldn't even get an address out of her, so I could look it up, or a phone number – I just had to follow instructions like, "Turn left here, and turn right there"!

'And I said, "Cor, she hasn't got any better!"'

'And Mike said, "You think that's bad – when we have to deliver stuff, she won't even give the address to delivery people either."'

'It's strange. She really works hard at keeping it private. It's great – to do that and just say "No" to all that, and interviews and all.'

With a full studio at her disposal Joan had been able to make clear demos of the songs. She also wrote out chord charts – but 'They're not always right!' says Phil. This may have been because she was still using eccentric guitar tunings. 'I think she writes a lot like that and then makes sense of it afterwards.'

The demos usually had guide vocals, but Joan was still reluctant to sing when everyone was there, partly because as producer she had to concentrate on what the band was playing.

'That made it slightly difficult,' says Jamie, 'because by the time you'd done half a dozen takes of the song without the vocal, you were concentrating so much on the chart that you tended to lose sight of what the actual song was about.' Sometimes they would then go back and listen to the demo, or Joan would put guide vocals on the main tape between sessions.

'She still does some strange things,' Phil remembers. 'There was one song that she hadn't finished the lyrics for. She had made a demo but there was no vocal on it. I decided it would be a good idea to know how the melody went, because it would change what I played – I didn't want to get in the way of the vocals, obviously. I asked her if she could just sing me the vocal. So she got up very close to my ear and whispered it to me – and everyone else is in the room, and she's very close to my ear and I'm giggling away! She wouldn't sing it again – that was my only chance! That's typical Joan.'

'The control room is absolutely huge,' says Dave Mattacks, 'and it's situated above what used to be a stable which she's had cleaned out. Knopfler and Pino [Palladino], the bass player, and the keyboard player and her were all upstairs in the control room and I was by myself downstairs ... with just a pair of cans. It's a great way to do it, because you've got complete separation. [Afterwards] everyone would tidy up the odd bar here and there. But basically it was all playing together, which was great.'

'Most time was spent on the feel of the tunes,' says Phil Palmer. 'All the ideas were coming from Joan, as they have to, but it was four or five good musicians knocking a song around and making it feel good.' Now that Joan had complete control she was prepared to relax that control.

'I would say she always knew what she wanted. Perhaps at that time she felt obliged to *bend* what she wanted by this all-powerful Glyn Johns figure. It's different now – she'll still *bend*, but it's not because she's been told to, it's because she realizes that *that* is an improvement. Especially the calibre of musician she's using these days – it's not as if she's just prepared to say, "This is what you play." She's expecting people to contribute something – and they do. And it works very well.

'Once you've bashed out the outline of the song, and the structure, light and shade, etc., once that's established, usually three or four takes maximum. Perhaps people patch up bits and pieces here and there.'

All her life Joan had been writing at the piano or on guitar. However, Graham Lyle, who played guitar on *Joan Armatrading*, went along to one of Joan's gigs in America and asked her if she ever writes with anybody.

'And I said, "No. Even when I wrote the first album and Pam Nestor did the lyrics, I've never worked *with* her, I've never sat down in a room with somebody. I just write it on the guitar or the piano."

'He said, "Have you ever tried working with a drum-machine?"

'And I said, "No."

'He said he started to do it and it's really good – you let the drum-machine dictate the rhythm and you'd be surprised at what will happen.

'So I thought, all right, Graham, and I went and bought myself this little machine and wrote "Living For You" on it.'

Of course, the basic drum patterns used when writing were not enough for the record. Drummer Jamie Lane had a suggestion.

'I think I introduced Joan to the concept of heavily programmed drums. "Living For You" was quite a slow track, the sort of thing that if you played it would sound a bit bland, MOR, but if you programmed it you get so much more artificial punch out of the drums that it makes a mid-tempo song like that live. So I suggested I should try programming it as if it was being played, then put on real high-hats and cymbals. And it worked very well. Since then I've done three more like that on the new album.'

One of the things Jamie Lane enjoyed about *The Shouting Stage* and the next album was the company. 'She always chooses great musicians. There was Pino Palladino on bass, who's wonderful, Phil Palmer on guitar, who's also tremendous, and Alan Clark on keyboards, which was a great bunch of people to be working with. This time it was Mick Karn from Japan on bass, and an American called Don Freeman on keyboards. It's really nice working with people of that calibre.'

Mark Knopfler had been a fan of Joan and she asked him to contribute. 'He's such a sensitive player,' she says, 'that he was adding things to the arrangement, and instead of me just saying, "I'd rather we'd stuck to my arrangement," I was really wishing I'd written them in the first place.

'There's one song called "Did I Make You Up" and everybody agreed that the song was sounding good, but it sounded like a lot of good musicians playing a good song, but nothing special. Then Mark went downstairs and he brought up a different electric guitar and nothing happened there, it still sounded like that. Then he went downstairs and got his acoustic guitar and sat down and immediately went *Riff!* – which is absolutely brilliant.'

'It was very interesting too,' says Dave Mattacks, 'because she knew exactly what she wanted – not so much what people played, but how the song was supposed to go. I remember a wonderful discussion between her and Knopfler – she was saying, "I really want it to go this way."

'He was saying, "Well, yes, but if you do that, it's going to go that way and it doesn't really work."

'She said, "No, that's really how I want it to go!"

'And he was saying, "But if you do that, that means..." And he ended up laughing and just saying, "You're strange!"

'But of course you hear the whole thing at the end and it all makes sense.

'It was interesting being away from her for the best part of eight or nine years and seeing just how much more confident she is. But not just an increase in confidence – an increase in knowing. It was an ideal situation inasmuch as you were working for someone who knows what they're doing, but gives you enough leeway to play what you want within the context of the song.'

Sometimes Joan played on the basic tracks but mostly she took the producer's role. Phil Palmer was surprised because 'She's got this ability to have an overall picture of the track before it's recorded, so she knows what she's gonna be putting on it. She can say, "Don't play there because there's going to be an acoustic guitar there." The normal way of doing it would be for her to play along or to sing, so people automatically know not to do something. But she tends not to do that. She's a one-off – that's the bottom line. I don't know anybody else like her. I don't ever expect to meet anyone else like her.

'When she started playing with electric guitar, she played it in the same way [as acoustic], and it doesn't work. Now she's got a bit more finesse – it is a different instrument. And she's playing a lot. In fact she's just finishing her new album and she's played all the guitars on it herself this time. And whether I'll get a call sometime, or someone will get a call to come and fix a few bits, I don't know. But she's quite confident about doing it now.

'She played a couple of solos on *The Shouting Stage* and you can tell it's her and it's a bit rough and ready but – it's her album.

'She tends to put too many effects on her guitars – for me. She'll plug an electric guitar through a dozen pedals, and it'll come out sounding really peculiar. But now she's got the ability to do it, she just likes to use everything that she can.'

Joan's final vocals were again recorded in seclusion, then she and Graham Dickson mixed the album at Olympic. Bumpkin Studios had produced a very classy result and A&M were well satisfied.

A single high-hat *tick* and we are enveloped in perfect sound – jazzy chords, easy hip-swaying rhythms, CD quality. 'The Devil I Know' is a good title, about the double standards some men have about being faithful. The lyric is sharp – 'Men/ No self control/ Says I'm all he wants/ But I watch him prowl/ Yet if I should stray/ I'm a wicked child' – but the mood and melody give little force to the words. There is one surprise here as Joan uses her own name in a song.

'Living For You' is very tropical sounding, with Guy Barker's high, easy trumpet and the synths ringing like a steel band. 'Your love has got me in a spin/ I turn around/ And I begin again' – and the song circles round and round.

The danger of using Mark Knopfler is that his style is so distinctive. On 'Did I Make You Up' it is good to hear him playing acoustic – but a far cry from Joan's old attack. Again it is a pleasure to hear the simplicity of Alan Clark's piano on 'Stronger Love'. Sweeping keyboards are used like the strings on *Joan Armatrading* and the song is very seventies, Laura Nyro, Joni Mitchell, Carole King. Stronger love is certainly one of Joan's main preoccupations, and the lack of trust is explored again in 'The Shouting Stage', very atmospheric and classy, again very CD, but with Joan's vocals casting back to Nina Simone.

Side two opens with a stronger, more distinctive song, 'Words', where Joan sings out as if she might indeed be 'desperate . . . to get back that feeling'. 'Straight Talk' pairs an accusing vocal with a calypso beat. This is interesting, but still seems to leave us missing the way the music and vocal intensity used to point up the mood on songs as different as 'Dry Land', 'Woncha Come On Home', 'Simon' and 'When I Get It Right'.

'Watch Your Step' has more urgency, but the words are unremarkable – 'There's people all around . . . they try to put us down . . . But I don't care what they say'. This lacks all the bite and originality of 'Kissin' And A Huggin'' or 'Taking My Baby Up Town'.

'All A Woman Needs' is another interesting idea. She told Paul Gambaccini: 'A group of us was having dinner and one woman was relating this story about a chap who really fancied this woman. And she'd say, "That's a nice handbag," and she'd have a handbag. Or she'd say, "I really like apples," and she'd get a crate of apples. Or, "I really like Lamborghinis," and there's the key. So she had to be a bit careful about what she said she liked! It was just a question of plying her with gifts, but he wasn't saying, "Well, I really like you," even. And when the woman was telling the story she actually used the words, "He says love will come later." Now to me, that's something to say to somebody.'

Finally on 'Dark Truths' a deep, echoy organ leads us into church, and Joan is 'afraid of dying/ Cos one day/ I'll find/ You're not forgiving.' This is an even stranger religious metaphor than 'Get In Touch With Jesus', but it is one way of conveying the power someone can have over you. Joan says this is one song where the music came first, 'and thinking very much of the arrangements'. It is quite short, and suddenly the album is over.

In some ways there is less to be said about the songs on this album than on any Joan has made. Just as the sound on *Joan Armatrading* was so lush that the music flowed over you, on this album not only is the sound smooth, the songs themselves are. To a certain extent Joan is re-examining old preoccupations, but without any sharp insights or new ideas. Of course it can be unfair to demand constant development or even continuing improvement, but this album seems to represent not just a mellowing but a turning away from challenge. Maybe Joan's own life is so relaxed now, her emotions so unruffled, that she *really* has to write about other people! Perhaps she has just had too much time to polish and repolish, leaving no rough edges – nothing to get to grips with.

Still, the album is excellent listening, the music lingers in the mind. Joan's voice, for all the CD smoothness, does work its way into the corners. As more albums follow, this may simply be seen as Joan taking an enjoyable holiday, a lightweight but successful exercise in jazzy soul.

The album cover is a very beautiful monochrome portrait, with Joan looking more wary than she has done since the earliest albums – collar turned up, eyes not meeting the close camera. The back cover features Joan's hands in a kind of sign language. Maybe if she had never learned to mistrust people we would not have had all this rich music and truthful poetry. It is a measure of Joan's stature and the standards she has set herself that an album as good as this should seem less than satisfying.

With *The Shouting Stage* released and doing respectably in the charts, Joan did some gentle promotion – a radio interview with Paul Gambaccini and a two-month tour. The show was very enjoyable, and it is no criticism to say it was predictable. Joan did what she does supremely well. The band also did very well – considering....

'I've always felt that Joan should be a little more adventurous with her bands,' says Phil Palmer. 'It comes down to finance too often. After *The Shouting Stage* we were asked if we wanted to tour. And we said, "Yes – I'd like to do it, if it wasn't too long."

'And they said, "Well, give us a figure – how much is it going to cost us?"

'And I put in a pretty reasonable figure. And they came back offering

me half of what I wanted. And I said, "I can't go and do it for that."
So – amicably – we decided I wouldn't do it.

'And I think the tour suffered because of it. The songs were so good
on *The Shouting Stage*, if she'd had a really hot band it would have
been a much more successful tour. She wasn't selling out places. The
word does get around. If Joan suffers from anything, I think it's that
area – management cutting corners. I was chatting to people who
have done more recent tours, and it's not been a happy experience for
her.'

In June the following year Joan made a solo appearance at the
Nelson Mandela seventieth birthday concert at Wembley Stadium.
Although Joan has been careful not to identify with black causes, this
was unquestionably close to her heart.

'I felt a lot of the people that were there were doing the concert for
the right reason – they were doing it in support of something. I will
only do things that I have some belief in. There are a lot of things you
can do that will promote your career, but I generally try and just do
the ones I think relate to me. The Nelson Mandela thing, yes obviously –
apartheid is definitely not the best way to conduct yourself, is it?'

Joan stepped on stage in the warm sun, relaxed and confident,
although singing with Midge Ure's band, not her own musicians. She
sang with great warmth the song everyone wanted to hear – 'Love
And Affection'. It came across that afternoon as a simple love song,
and the boisterous crowd of seventy thousand responded. Joan seemed
to be opening up as never before, a mature and contented woman.

Tracy Chapman, in contrast, was obviously a very shy, nervous and
inexperienced girl, unknown to most of the crowd, who practically
ignored her solo sets as they talked and went for ice-creams and drinks.
They were mostly young, white, and into heavier rock. But through
the intimacy of the television camera Tracy came across vividly to
millions around the world. The inattentive crowd was unheard and
simply appeared as a thronged stadium as the helicopter camera
zoomed up and Tracy sang of revolution.

To many, Tracy Chapman's gain has been Joan Armatrading's loss,
but comparisons here are a little too easy. After all, how many black,
women singer-songwriters can we compare? Of course Tracy Chapman
has heard Joan Armatrading records and of course the influence is
there – and there to be heard. But then their voices are similar, whereas

Joan's influences were Joni Mitchell, Carole King, Elton John and later Van Morrison. If Joan and Nina Simone had shared the same bill at a big concert, then comparisons would have been drawn. And if, at the beginning of her career, Joan had been able to appear at a big festival beamed around the world by satellite television, then maybe she too would have had tearaway record sales to match the reviews she was getting.

Joan may have regrets, she may even resent Tracy Chapman's sudden success. It must be significant that Joan has *not* heard her first album.

'When I was mixing my album she came on the video thing and they all called me out and said, "You've got to watch this!" But I only heard a couple of bars and you can't tell from that. I've never heard a record.

'I'm not being difficult. I don't feel that kind of curiosity. If she sounds like me then I've heard me and I know what I sound like. But I must say that never before have so many people said that someone sounds like me – my decorator, friends, people in shops.'

There are strong parallels to be drawn between Tracy Chapman now and Joan Armatrading then. Descriptions of Tracy's gigs read like Joan's first appearance at Ronnie Scott's. The professional profile is very similar – she is intensely private, shuns publicity and gives no interviews. But for most people the significant fact is that Tracy sounds like Joan used to – and therefore the way many fans wish Joan still sounded. Mike Howlett and Gus Dudgeon both feel Joan should record an acoustic album – but would an acoustic album repeat the success of *Joan Armatrading*?

Joan is not one to ignore commercial success. Comparing *Joan Armatrading* with her previous albums, she has said, 'The big thing that made it so much better for me was the fact that it sold.' Joan doesn't really want nineteen cars, and she can get to China or Japan by arranging a tour or buying a ticket. What Joan wants is to be able to write and record *what* she wants, *when* she wants, and probably *with whom* she wants. For this she must continue to be as successful as she has been, and there is no reason to doubt that she will. If Joan made an acoustic album now, it might outsell the others. But it would be sad if her heart wasn't in it. Perhaps she will record that album when people have stopped urging her to do so.

Meanwhile Joan made a move in that direction – the Channel 4 programme *Acoustic* filmed at her home, the beautiful, old, white-walled, red-tiled country house. The diplomatic – not to say ambassadorial – Paul Gambaccini again conducted the interviews and we were treated to a number of songs from *The Shouting Stage* complete with studio musicians, plus Joan's solo acoustic rendering of some oldies ('Child Star' and 'Call Me Names') and her idol Van Morrison's 'Moondance'. Joan explained how teaching herself guitar produced her unique style.

'When I got my guitar, I knew what happened in music so I used to try and play all the bits. That's why I started rhythmic, because I would try and play the bass line, and try and play the rhythm and put the drum fills in. When I did my first album, playing with musicians for the first time, they had a job because I was everywhere! Not leaving them much room!'

There was a surprising encounter when Elton John dropped in to accompany Joan on 'Stronger Love'. He also remembered Joan making the first album and how his favourite song was 'It Could Have Been Better'.

'Elton John is my favourite live artist,' Joan told us. 'He's the person I've seen the most in concert. I've seen him numerous times in England, and only ever managed to see him abroad once, which was in Australia, and he's never let me down.'

In 1989 Joan started on the next album. Drummer Jamie Lane was once again working with her.

'I believe on the current album there's a lot more of her guitar playing.' There is no let-up in the technical side and Jamie has followed up his machine work on 'Living For You'. 'Some of the tracks were machine-based tracks and they were built up one by one. On this album it's being programmed in that way. Not all the tracks, but on some of the seemingly more commercial, more single-orientated ones, she likes the directness – this strength of programmed percussion on it works nicely. I think there's some very good songs on the upcoming album. It would be great if Joan could establish herself again with a hit single, and I think there's one might do that.'

Joan continues to play occasional one-off live gigs. Steve Greetham saw her in the 1987 Prince's Trust concert. 'She performed a couple of tracks off *Sleight Of Hand* with a fairly all-star band and I was quite chuffed to see Mark King playing my bass parts. She looked good doing that.' And she had the courage to play a solo with Clapton and Knopfler in the wings!

'First and foremost,' says Steve, 'I think she was always a musician, and she always felt that she was on a par with all her contemporaries. She talks to Townsend and Clapton, and people like this all the time, and Phil Collins – she's in the Prince's Trust. And rightly so. But unfortunately she never got that kind of recognition for doing it.'

Joan did get to play an unusual gig in Africa as a result. Phil Palmer flew out there.

'It was Swaziland – the king's birthday. He decided that the Prince's Trust was a very good idea, and that he should do something similar himself. So he decided to put this concert on – it's gonna be a yearly event now. It's a wonderful, wonderful place – a big football stadium, surrounded by mountains. Joan was very happy, she just did it on her own – acoustic guitar. And we all went to visit the king.

'There was a great picture – I wish I'd had a camera on me – Joan and the king sitting next to each other on these big chairs, almost thrones, and Joan's feet weren't touching the ground. It was very sweet!'

Joan may not have nineteen cars, but there are over twenty horses in residence at a local stud farm she has bought, a twenty-eight acre spread near Hindhead, not far from her house and studio. The stud is run for her by a professional groom as Joan is still learning about horses.

'Complete idiot really! I don't know anything about horses – four legs and a tail and a head, that's it. But I started to set up the stud farm hopefully to be a proper sort of business and not just a game. For some reason I got into it, and once you're in it, there's no stopping, because you start to look at the animals as if they're people.'

Joan was being interviewed by Sue Lawley on BBC's *Desert Island Discs*. Needless to say, the prospect of being marooned on an island did not worry her.

'Oh, I'd love it! When I go on tour my favourite time is after the show when I've played in front of thousands of people – which is brilliant, I love that – when I go to my room, and it's just me on my own, and maybe watching a bit of television or something. I wouldn't particularly miss people. I wouldn't miss the television. I wouldn't miss the radio. I wouldn't necessarily miss having a car cos I like to walk anyway.' When at home Joan often gets up at 6 a.m. and walks ten miles a day in the woods and fields.

'When I'm writing I'm pretty much on my own – I have to be. But once I've done whatever work I want to do there and I go up to the farm, then it's nice.'

'You're a very disciplined person, aren't you? You don't smoke, you don't drink, you're a vegetarian – so in all this, how do you get your kicks?'

Joan laughed. 'I dunno – I just enjoy doing whatever I do. I read my comics – *The Dandy*, *The Beano*, *Mandy*, *Bunty*, *Judy*, *Whoopi*, *Whizzer and Chips*, *Barky* – when that used to come out – *Topper*, *Beezer*, you name it, I'll read it. There's a black Superman in the African comics, so I try and get different things.' (Joan also reads *Viz Comic*, a favourite character being Sid the Sexist.)

Sue Lawley asked: 'What is there left for Joan Armatrading to do? Are you still ambitious for something?'

'Yes, it's still for my work – me and every other songwriter trying to write the song that will last forever. You know – in a hundred years' time they'll be playing whatever this song is.'

'Some would say perhaps you did thirteen years ago when you wrote "Love And Affection"?'

'Yeah, "Love And Affection" is a good song, I have to be honest about this, and they're still playing it today. Yes. And when I sing it, ever since I wrote it I've sung it at every concert, and I have no problems singing it.'

Joan's desert island 'luxury' would be her guitar, of course, and she asked for an Agatha Christie novel. Radio Four is certainly Joan Armatrading's style with its educated, middle-class discussion programmes, plays, interviews and documentaries. She hardly knows what's in the top ten. More relaxed now, she thoroughly enjoys working, and when she's not working she follows the rural life – gardening, visiting horse shows and traction-engine rallies.

'I think I've finally owned up that I don't have to keep proving myself. I've got a picture in my studio of the front cover of *Melody Maker* with the Bay City Rollers – and I'm still here...!'

Postscript

Is Joan in love? *Hearts And Flowers* is all about love, and Joan seems to be up to her neck – and revelling in it! This is a confident, exuberant album, one of her strongest for years, both musically and lyrically. Joan has produced a danceable and intelligent set – and played all the guitars herself!

The album opens on a low key with the single, 'More Than One Kind Of Love'. It introduces us immediately to the album's most consistent sound, the bell-like keyboards of American Don Freeman. It also features Jamie Lane's heavily programmed drums, busy but unobtrusive, keeping a constant pulse going under Joan's steady voice.

The message here is the antithesis – or an answer – to the doubts of 'Love And Affection'. Then, it was 'with friends I still feel/so insecure', but now she is saying, 'remember your friends' and 'Good friendships never die'.

The title track 'Hearts And Flowers' follows, a breezy, sentimental love song with Joan singing in octaves. She is playing guitar and keyboards, cheerfully raiding the synth library of sounds – Angel Voices and Chinese Wood Blocks – but economically and to great effect. On this and on 'Can't Let Go' she plays all the instruments, 'alone' again for the first time since the first two albums. There are no drums on these numbers, yet they are very rhythmic – unusual perpetual-motion exercises in jogging keyboards with strong overtones of

Philip Glass. This whole album is very rhythmic – but not 'slave to the rhythm'. These are songs to dance to, not disco tracks.

'Promise Land' opens with Joan's steady acoustic guitar and Mick Karn duetting on bass, building up a marvellous suspense as we await Steve Jansen's explosive drum entry — a series of big 'fills' which never settle into a regular dram part, Joan has not forgotten Steve Lillywhite and gated echo, but the number belongs more to the sixties with its soul/gospel beat and high 'morse code' piano octaves.

'Someone's In The Background' is darker, both musically and in its jealous, paranoid fear of that 'someones else' – *alter ego* or rival lover? But it is also witty – musically and lyrically – with bizarre percussion overlaying the basic pounding beat. This number and 'Something In The Air Tonight' are both very 'Prince' in their economy of style. With the bland smoothness of *The Shouting Stage* behind her, Joan is using her voice percussively to kick the words along, emphasizing the mood, and the number finishes with a swirling 'out of control' sax solo from Andy Shepherd.
bravely unaccompanied funky beat for the obsessive 'Can't Let Go'.

'Free' opens side two confidently with Joan's urgent acoustic, another energetic, gospel-based number which builds to a soaring rock sax solo. 'Something in The Air' swings in like Bowie's 'Golden Years' or Jimi Hendrix's 'All Along The Watchtower' and soon becomes a delicious carnival as Joan throws in exotic percussion and Latin synth-brass. 'Always' is a simple love song with Don Freeman's sensitive accompaniment. 'Good Times' has Joan returning to the tough blues roots she first displayed on 'Mean Old Man' – this time throwing in a Heavy Metal solo for good measure. 'The Power Of Dreams' rounds the album off with one of Joan's measured, hymn-like songs.

This is the nearest she has ever come to a concept album, and the title says it all – and without irony. It is Joan's paean to love, wholeheartedly embracing the ups and the downs. Every song here is about love and the subject could easily be one person and a single relationship. The songs virtually chart the course of it.

'More than One Kind Of Love' is the warning before she plunges headlong into love. 'Hearts And Flowers' is the first sweet blossoming, and she turns to us and says – in reply to the doubts – 'People ... I know you think I'm foolish/And I'm making a mistake but/To me this is perfect'. Then it's 'Yes I'm ready to take your hand/Follow you into the promise land'. For the first time Joan is prepared to put her complete trust in someone.

The next four songs deal with the down side – the jealousy, the obsession, the break up, the recriminations – but Joan now has the strength to bear all this. There is no 'victim' song, no 'Oh! how I'm suffering'. In 'Someone's In The Background' it's 'Put 'em on the phone right now' – Joan is ready to deal with the competition. 'Can't Let Go' keeps repeating 'Darling' and reaffirms 'We may argue and fight . . . But . . . we belong/In each other's arms'. In 'Free' she is 'giving you your freedom' with confidence, and her mood is 'up'. In 'Something In The Air Tonight' she accuses 'How could you hide your love away from me', but there is no sense of just allowing this to happen – there's too much energy in the song!

It would be simplistic to say that 'Always' is making up after the break up – this is not a musical – but the last three songs reaffirm three important sides of love and do so in more positive terms than Joan is wont to use. 'Good Times' is the most physical we have heard her and the muscular blues hammers this home. 'The Power Of Dreams' again casts doubt aside – 'You supply/All the answers . . . Your honest emotions . . . All disillusions/Were shattered . . . The strength of a new love/Can conquer all'.

The music confirms this mood, with Joan using the full range of her voice. There is a strong feeling of musical roots here and echoes of her earlier albums, particularly *Back To The Night*. She uses small, tasty bands, plays more herself, and keeps a tight rein on the bubbling energy. This may not be an album of classics, but it is her most exciting for a long time and melts any doubts about Joan as an important and still-developing artist. The years of success have not sapped her creativity.

Is Joan in love? Oh, yes – and she is obviously in love with life.

Chronology

This Chronology is an informal guide only. As this is an unofficial biography I have been unable to confer with Joan Armatrading's management or record company.

1950
9 December 1950. Joan born in Basseterre, St Kitts, West Indies to Amos Ezekiel Armatrading and Beryl Agatha, née Benjamin.

Father was a carpenter and played in a band.

1954
Joan's parents and two older brothers move to Birmingham, England, leaving Joan with grandparents on nearby Antigua.

1958
Joan joins her family in Stetchford, Birmingham. They live in one room at 22 Coralie Street, Birmingham 18. Mr Armatrading is employed as a bus driver.

1960
Sister Jacqueline born.

1961
Brother Tony born.

1962
Canterbury Cross Secondary Modern. Often absent looking after mother when she was ill. 'I wasn't very good at school but I did play the recorder a bit and sang in the choir.'

1963
Brother Andrew born.

1964
Starts to teach herself piano and later guitar.

Writes song 'for Marianne Faithful' – 'When I Was Young'.

1966
One night Joan's father throws her out and she stays for a while with

her brother's girlfriend. Returns but knows she'll leave again.

Leaves school to earn her living. For a short time works comptometer machine in an office.

Forms duo with schoolfriend Scott gigging around local clubs.

1968
Auditions in Birmingham for the Afro Asian Caribbean Agency and then in London for *Hair*. Joins the national touring company. Meets Pam Nestor. They start to write songs together.

1969
Moves to London, lives in room in West Hampstead. Continues writing with Pam Nestor. They both join music/dance group Dice formed from members of *Hair*.

1971
Pam and Joan take demos to Essex Music. In due course Mike Noble hears the tape and plays it to Gus Dudgeon who signs them for Tuesday Productions.

1972
Gus Dudgeon records demos at Marquee Studios with Larry Steele (bass), Caleb Quaye (guitar) and Roger Pope (drums).

First album recorded at Strawberry Studios, Château d'Herouville, France.

November. *Whatever's For Us* (Hifly 12) released on Cube records, excellent reviews. It sells only 2,000 copies.

First appearance at Ronnie Scott's with Henry Spinetti (drums) Joe Partridge (guitar) and Larry Steele. Joan parts company with Pam Nestor.

7 December. Joan opens for the JSD band (folk) at the Fairfield Halls in Croydon.

1973
European tour with José Feliciano.

April. Two-week residency at Ronnie Scott's club Upstairs.

June. 'Lonely Lady'/'Together In Words And Music' BUG31 producer Gus Dudgeon; *Melody Maker* and *Sounds* reviews.

Solo tour of USA folk clubs.

1974
Joan fights for release from Cube contract.

1975
Joan signs to A&M Records (Britain). Records album *Back To The Night* with Pete Gage at Rockfield Studio (Wales) and Basing Street Studios (London).

17 April. Joan plays at her launch party at London's Playboy Club with The Movies – J. Cole (guitar) Greg Knowles (steel guitar) Jamie Lane (drums) Durban Laverde (bass) Dag Small (keyboard, clarinet).

May. *Back To The Night* AMLH 68305.

'Back To The Night' AMS 7181.

2 May. BBC *Old Grey Whistle Test* with Doctor Hook.

June. Joan appears at Hyde Park free festival.

August. Successful fortnight at Ronnie Scott's with The Movies.

US tours supporting Nils Lofgren, Supertramp, with The Movies. One hundred gigs in one hundred days.

November. Support on British Supertramp tour.

1976
'Dry Land' AMS 7205.

2 August. *Joan Armatrading* AMLH 64588.

No. 12 UK No. 67 US.

US Tour with Jerry Donahue (guitars), Pat Donaldson (bass), Dave Mattacks (drums) plus Albert Lee (guitar keyboard) for later gigs.

September. US tour supporting Richie Havens.

18 September. *Joan Armatrading* enters LP chart at No. 30.

23 September. Joan and band interrupt US tour to fly back for Hammersmith Odeon – special gig, supported by Moon. A sell-out.

October. 'Love And Affection' AMS 7249 peaks at No. 10.

BBC TV *Top Of The Pops*.

2 October. Joan returns to tour the States supporting Stephen Stills.

5 October. BBC TV *Old Grey Whistle Test*: 'Down To Zero', 'Love And Affection'.

6 November. 'Love And Affection' enters charts at No. 20.

4 December. BBC TV *Michael Parkinson Show*.

British Tour.

25 December. *Sounds* front page picture and best album of 1976 (Joni Mitchell *Hejira* No. 2, *Royal Scam* Steely Dan No. 3, Bob Dylan *Desire* No. 4).

Living in a flat in Surbiton.

'Down To Zero'/'Like Fire' AMS 7270.

This year Decca re-released LP *Whatever's For Us* and 'Alice' as a single.

1977
July. *Joan Armatrading* goes gold.

11 September. *Show Some Emotion* AMLH 68433 No. 6 UK No. 52 US.

'Show Some Emotion' AMS 7331.

23 September. 'Willow' AMS 7316.

5 October. BBC TV *Old Grey Whistle Test*.

British Tour: Jerry Donahue guitar, Bryan Garafolo (bass), Red Young (keyboards), Quitman Dennis (horns), Dave Kemper (drums).

Derek Jewell (who wrote *Sunday Times* review in 1972) plays tracks from *Show Some Emotion* on *Sounds Interesting*.

3–4 November. Hammersmith Odeon (sold out) – filmed for BBC TV *Sight & Sound* (Joan hates film – 1978 interview).

Hammersmith Odeon extra show.

Latest album sells over 150,000 and stays twenty-five weeks in US chart.

1978
'Warm Love' AMS 7346.

Touring Australia, New Zealand, Canada, Europe.

July. 'Flight Of The Wild Geese'/'No Way Out' AMS 7365. Joan heckled at première.

15 July Bob Dylan's 'Picnic' at Blackbushe Aerodrome (in Hampshire), Camberley, Surrey: Bob Dylan, Eric Clapton, Graham Parker and The Rumour, Lake – 250,000 people. (Joan breaks off Australasian tour for this gig).

24 July. *To The Limit* AMLH 64732, No. 13.

'Bottom To The Top' AMS 7393.

1979
Joan sues A&M for $10m.

US Tour – used for live LP.

European Tour.

March. British Tour: Red Young (keyboards), Ricky Hirsh (guitar), Bill Bodine (bass), Art Rodriguez (drums), Lon Price (saxophone) (support: George Duke).

12,13 March. Wembley Arena – two shows.

'Taking My Baby Uptown' AMS 77422.

July. Pam Nestor single: 'Hiding & Seeking (No More)'/'Man On The Run' Chrysalis CHS 2349, producers Ken Cumberbatch/Dennis Bovell, Essex Music.

October. *Steppin' Out* (Live) AMLH 64789.

Rest of world tour – autumn and winter.

EP released in US: 'Rosie', 'How Cruel', 'He Wants Her', 'I Really Must Be Going'.

Operation in Australia – cyst removed, three months recuperating.

1980
February. 'Rosie'/'How Cruel' AMS 7506 No. 49.

April–August. European and American tour of eleven countries (twenty-nine cities).

20 April. BBC 2: *Rock Over Europe* – German TV *Rockpalast* screened to Western and Eastern Europe including Russia.

12 May. *Me Myself I* AMLH 64809 reaches No. 5.

May. British Tour: Dickie Sims (keyboards), Bill Bodine (bass), Ricky Hirsh (guitar), Rick Beilke (guitar), Richie Hayward (drums).

June 'Me Myself I' (single) No. 21.

Summer. Joan records *Walk Under Ladders* 'Take 1' in New York with Richard Gottehrer, Anton Fig and Chris Spedding. Joan and A&M decide it must be re-done with session musicians.

July. Tours Canada.

August. Tours US.

September. 'All The Way From America'/'Is It Tomorrow Yet' AMS 7552 No. 54.

28 September. Interview with Mike Sparrow on BBC Radio London's *Breakthrough*.

October. Final British Tour dates.

October–November. Steve Lillywhite records *Walk Under Ladders* 'Take 2' at the Town House.

1981
Minor operation in London.

21 August. 'I'm Lucky'/'Shine' AMS 8163 No. 46.

4 September. *Walk Under Ladders* AMLH 64876 reaches No. 6.

October. Minor operation causes postponement of British tour from October to December.

December. 12–15 Hammersmith Odeon.

Living in quiet detached house near Kingston-upon-Thames. Takes up fishing; drives Honda.

1982
January. 'No Love' AMS 8179 No. 50.

June. 'Lonely Lady' Cube Records.

30 August. In Concert on BBC 2 – recorded in Boston earlier in the year.

1983
February. 'Drop The Pilot' AMS 8306 No. 11 UK, No. 78 US.

7 March. 'The Key'.

14 March. *The Key* AMLX 64912 No. 10 UK, No. 32 US.

British Tour. Band: Phil Palmer (guitar), Ian Maidman (bass), Mike Simmonds (keyboards), Julian Diggle (percussion), Justin Hildreth (drums).

6, 7 April. Wembley Arena.

25 March. European Tour.

17 June. US Tour.

August. Canadian Tour.

9 September. Australia and New Zealand Tour.

Japanese tour cancelled.

15 September. Joan does show for St Kitts Independence Day (19 September) at Warner Park (solo).

'Call Me Names'/'For The Best'.

21 November. *Track record* LP and Video.

1984
12 May. 'Who's That Girl' interview on BBC Radio 1 with Janice Long.

4–17 September. High Court case against ex-manager Mike Stone to nullify a 1976 five-year contract. Successful, but later damages waived.

11 September. BBC 2 *Late Night in Concert* shows (filmed in Sydney, Australia previous year).

1985
4 February. *Secret Secrets* AMA 5040 No. 14 UK, No. 73 US.
February. 'Temptation'.

10 February. British Tour: Armatouring '85.

Tour Band: Lee Davison (guitar), Steve Greetham (bass), Mark Parnell (drums), Alex White (keyboards), Jim Ross (saxophone), Ted Emmett (trumpet); tour managers Pat King, Stewart Grant.

1–6 March. Hammersmith Odeon.

9 March. European Tour.

4 April. BBC 2 and Radio 1 *Into the Music* in concert.

1 May. US Tour.

1 May. 'Thinking Man' AM 250.

7 June. Australian Tour.

British Tour, Canada, Israel, Australia – given key to city of Sydney.

3 August. BBC TV show of 1983 Australian tour.

September. Israel, open-air gig at Tel Aviv.

1986
Joan living in house in Surrey with recording studio (Bumpkin Studios), upgraded from 16- to 24-track.

April. 'Kind Words (And A Real Good Heart') AM 315.

5 April. Comic Relief at Shaftesbury Theatre.

8 May. *Sleight Of Hand* AMA 5130 No. 38.

June. 'Reach Out' AM 338.

September. 'Jesse'/'Don Juan'/'Love And Affection' AM 350.

December. Collapses at end of Australian tour so decides to take a year off.

1987
Takes this year off.

Prince's Trust concert with Knopfler and Clapton.

December. Joan buys 28-acre stud farm near Hindhead, not far from her country house.

1988
11 June. Wembley Stadium: Joan appears in Nelson Mandela seventieth birthday concert.

29 June. *The Shouting Stage* AMA 5211.

July. 'The Shouting Stage'/'I Really Must Be going'/'He Wants Her' AM 449.

August. 'Living For You'/'Innocent Request' AM 460.

Channel 4 programme *Acoustic* filmed 'at home'.

August. British Tour: Mick Daitch (guitar), Bob Noble (keyboards), Jeremy Meek (bass), James Ross (saxophone), John Nicolson (drums).

1–3 October. London, Hammersmith Odeon.

November. 'Stronger Love'/'The Devil I know'.

1989
29 January. BBC Radio 4 *Desert Island Discs*. Mendelssohn's Violin Concerto, Ella FitzGerald 'That Old Black Magic', Van Morrison 'Madame George', Mahler's Symphony No. 4 in G major, *The Magnificent Seven* theme music, Verdi's *Requiem*, Muddy Waters 'I'm A Man' and Dvořák's New World Symphony.

13 February. Presents special BPI award to Phil Collins.

1990
7 May. New releases:
7″ single and cassette: 'More Than One Kind Of Love'/'Love And Affection' (live at Hammersmith, Oct 88)

5″ CD 'More Than One Kind Of Love'/'Good Times' (from new album)/'Love And Affection' (live at Hammersmith, Oct 88)/'I'm Lucky' (live at Hammersmith, Oct 88) 12″ single – same tracks as CD.

11 May. Joan performs 'More Than One Kind Of Love' live on *Wogan*.

16 May. Joan performs 'More Than One Kind Of Love' live on TVAM.

4 June. New album release – *Hearts And Flowers*.

24 June. UK tour opens at Birmingham Hippodrome.

8, 9 July. UK tour ends with two nights at Hammersmith Odeon.

6 August. US tour opens at Saratoga.

14–16 August. New York, Beacon Theatre.

22, 23 August. Los Angeles, Wiltern Theatre.

25 August. US tour ends at Berkeley.

Discography

This Discography is an informal guide as I have been unable to check the information with A&M records.

WHATEVER'S FOR US
  Hifly 12   Nov 72
    Producer: Gus Dudgeon
My Family (Armatrading/Nestor)
City Girl (Armatrading)
Spend A Little Time (Armatrading)
Whatever's For Us (A/N)
Child Star (A/N)
Visionary Mountains (A/N)
It Could Have Been Better (A/N)
Head Of The Table (A/N)
Mister Remember Me (A/N)
Gave it a try (A/N)
Alice (A/N)
Conversation (A)
Mean Old Man (A/N)
All The Kings' Gardens (A/N)

Lonely Lady/
  Together In Words & Music
    BUG 31   June 73

BACK TO THE NIGHT
  AMLH 68305   May 75

    Producer: Pete Gage
No Love For Free
Travelled So Far
Steppin' Out
Dry Land (Armatrading/Nestor)
Cool Blue Stole My Heart
Get In Touch With Jesus
Body To Dust
Back To The Night
So Good
Let's Go Dancing
Come When You Need Me (A/N)

Back To The Night
    AMS 7181

Dry Land (Armatrading/Nestor)
    AMS 7205

JOAN ARMATRADING
    AMLH 64588   Aug 76
      Producer: Glyn Johns
Down To Zero
Help Yourself

Water With The Wine
Love And Affection
Save Me
Join The Boys
People
Somebody Who Loves You
Like Fire
Tall In The Saddle

Love And Affection
  AMS 7249   Oct 76

Down To Zero
  AMS 7270

SHOW SOME EMOTION
  AMLH 68433   Sept 77
  Producer: Glyn Johns
Woncha Come On Home
Show Some Emotion
Warm Love
Never Is Too Late
Peace In Mind
Opportunity
Mama Mercy
Get In The Sun
Willow
Kissin' And A Huggin'

Show Some Emotion
  AMS 7331

Willow
  AMS 7316   Sept 77

Warm Love
  AMS 7346   78

**Flight Of The Wild Geese/
No Way Out**
  AMS 7365   July 78

TO THE LIMIT
  AMLH 64732   July 78
  Producer: Glyn Johns
Barefoot And Pregnant

Your Letter
Am I Blue For You
You Rope You Tie Me
Baby I
Bottom To The Top
Taking My Baby Up Town
What Do You Want
Wishing
Let It Last

Bottom To The Top AMS 7393

Taking My Baby Up Town 7422

STEPPIN' OUT (Live)
  AMLH 64789   Oct 79
  Producer: Glyn Johns
Mama Mercy
Cool Blue Stole My Heart
How Cruel
Love Song
Love And Affection
Steppin' Out
You Rope You Tie Me
Kissin' And A Huggin'
Tall In The Saddle

Rosie/How Cruel AMS 7506

ME MYSELF I
  AMLH 64809   May 80
  Producer: Richard Gottehrer
Me Myself I
Ma-Me-O-Beach
Friends
Is It Tomorrow Yet
Turn Out The Light
When You Kisses Me
All the Way From America
Feeling In My Heart (For You)
Simon
I Need You

Me Myself I

All the Way From America

WALK UNDER LADDERS
    AMLH 64809   Aug 81
    Producer: Steve Lillywhite
I'm Lucky
When I Get It Right
Romancers
I Wanna Hold You
The Weakness In Me
No Love
At The Hop
I Can't Lie To Myself
Eating The Bear
Only One

I'm Lucky   AMS 8163

No Love

THE KEY
    AMLX 64912   Mar 83
    Producer: Steve Lillywhite
Call Me Names
Foolish Pride
Drop The Pilot
The Key
Everybody Gotta Know
Tell Tale
What Do Boys Dream
The Dealer
Bad Habits
I Love My Baby

Call Me Names/For The Best
    AM 116

Drop The Pilot

The Key

TRACK RECORD
    JA 2001   Nov 83
Drop The Pilot
(I Love It When You) Call Me Names
Frustration
When I Get It Right
I'm Lucky

Me Myself I
The Weakness In Me
Heaven
Down To Zero
Love And Affection
Show Some Emotion
Willow
Rosie

SECRET SECRETS
    AMA 5040   Feb 85
    Producer: Mike Howlett
Persona Grata
Temptation
Moves
Talking To The Wall
Love By You
Thinking Man
Friends Not Lovers
One Night
Secret Secrets
Strange

Thinking Man

SLEIGHT OF HAND
    AMA 5130   May 86
    Producer: Joan Armatrading
Kind Words (And A Real Good Heart)
Killing Time
Reach Out
Angelman
Laurel And The Rose
One More Chance
Russian Roulette
Jesse
Figure Of Speech
Don Juan

Kind Words (And A Real Good Heart)

THE SHOUTING STAGE
    AMA 5211   June 88
    Producer: Joan Armatrading
The Devil I Know
Living For You

Did I Make You Up
Stronger Love
The Shouting Stage
Words
Straight Talk
Watch Your Step
All A Woman Needs
Dark Truths

The Devil I Know

Living For You   AM 460

More Than One Kind Of Love/
Love And Affection (Live)
(and on 12″ and CD) **Good Times/**

I'm Lucky (live)
   AMY 561   May 90

HEARTS AND FLOWERS
   395298–1   June 90
   Producer: Joan Armatrading
More Than One Kind Of Love
Hearts And Flowers
Promise Land
Someone's In The Background
Can't Let Go
Free
Something In The Air Tonight
Always
Good Times
The Power Of Dreams

All the A&M albums are still on release and also available on CD. The first album, Whatever's For Us, has been reissued on Castle Classics (Unit 7, 271 Merton Road, London SW18 5JS) on LP and CD.

Main Index

(Ch refers to chapters)

Armatrading, Joan
  bass 7 29 116 145
  cars 66 75 87 91 113 146
  clothes 7 8 24 25 29 33 51
    56 67 72 92 133 146
  drum machine 141 151+
  family Ch1 22 125+
  food 13 25 35 75 91 102
    113 119 129+ 137
    145+ 149
  friends 13 26 75
  guitar 4 6 7 14 19 29 34
    37 38 49 57 59 62 70
    77 96 100 106 107 109
    116 117 123 126 130
    138 141 142 143 153
    157 160 161+
  homes 3 13 33 86 91 103
    113 125 128 145 148+
    159
  interviews 25 26 50 66
    67+ 75+ 81 88+
    91+ 93+ 119 127 145
    150 159
  keyboard 103+ 141 145
    161+
  live performance 6 7 14 20
    50+ 52 70 81+ 90+
    103 136
  management:
  see Miles Copeland, Mike
    Noble, John Sherry, Mike
    Stone

piano 3 4 11 14 21 36 38
  52 101 107
vocals 17 23 24 40 41+
  61 78 107 111 131 133
  137 142 150
writing 4 5 6 8 29 30+ 33
  38 39 45 46 57+ 62
  67+ 79+ 81 92 93
  98+ 102 107 114 127
  138+ 140 145 151 154
  160
Armatrading, Amos (father) 1
  4 5 22 66 93
Armatrading, Andrew
  (brother) 3 85 93
Armatrading, Beryl (mother)
  1 2 5 6 93
Armatrading, Jacqueline
  (sister) 3 93
Armatrading, Tony (brother)
  3 93 144
Armatrading, elder brothers 1
  5 6
Abba 116+
Acoustic 158
Africa 159
Afro Asian Caribbean Agency
  7 12
A&M Records 29 31 38 46+
  53 66 70 71 95 105 106
  116 118 119 122 131
  135 140 153
America – see USA

Anderle, David 90
Anti Nazi League 95
Antigua 1 126
Arrowsmith, Clive 47
Atlantic Records 23
Auditions 7 135
Australia 96 123 125 136
  138 146

Barker, Guy 117 153
Bass 44 53 57 59+ 129 135
  141 162 (see also under
  Armatrading)
Basseterre 1
Bay City Rollers 160 (photo)
BBC 29 73 82 116 127 159
The Beano 8 66 119 122 160
Beilke, Rick 103
Belew, Adrian 117+ 119
  120 144
Bell, Edward 112
Bentley, Steve 91
The Best of Joan Armatrading
  112
Betten, Matt 91
The Bible, religion 23 45 134
  154
Birmingham 2+ 66 103
Bitteli, Dave 132
Black Echoes 88+ 93 (photo)
Blackbushe 90+ 95
Blondie 98
Blue 45

Bodine, Bill 103
Bowie, David 17 84 112
    117+ 120 162
Brooks, Elkie 32 35 46 47 53
Brown, Steve 108
Burfield, Tony 33
Bush, Kate 119 146

Canada 102
Chapman, Tracy 156+
Charone, Barbara 50
Chen, Phil 39
Christie, Agatha 160
Clapton, Eric 17 90 159
Clark, Alan 154
Clemons, Clarence 99 144
Clubs 7 29 – Bottom Line 52
    69, Cellar Door 56,
    Manzil Room 123,
    Playboy 49, Ritz 137,
    Ronnie Scott's 26 27+
    48 50+ 74 157
Coleman, Ray 80
Collins, Mel 117
Collins, Phil 108 120 159
Comics 76 93 119 160 (see
    Beano)
Connor, Edric 7
Conway, Gerry Ch3 18+ 27
Coon, Caroline 43 67+
Cooper, Ray 18
Copeland, Miles 26 116
Copeland, Stewart 29 116
Coronation Street 92 127
Cube records 25 28 31
Cumberbach, Ken 30

'Darkness' 12
Davison, Les 135 146+
Decca 73
Demos 14 17 36 53 98 103+
    106 117 127 128+
    140+ 145 150
Denmark Street 12
Dennis, Quitman 81 83 87 91
Desert Island Discs 14 159
Dice 13 17
Dickson, Graham 149, 153
Diggle, Julian 49 121
Dinah's Café 30
Dolby, Thomas 108+ 114+
    117 121
D'Oliviera, Raoul 132
Donahue, Jerry 54 57+ 60
    67 69 77 81
Donaldson, Pat 67 70 79

Drum-machine – see Linn and
    under Armatrading
Drums 59 77+ 85+ 100
    106 108+ 130 141
    161+
Dudgeon, Gus Ch3 16+ 19
    26 28 31 50 57 113
    149+ 157
Dugmore, Geoff 142+ 146
Dunbar, Sly 40 107 112
Dylan, Bob 6 23 74 90

Emmit, Ted 135+
Engineers 16 21 132+ 141
    149
Essex Music 14 16+ 20 53
    122
E Street Band 99

Fairport Convention 57 67
Faithful, Marianne 4
Fast, Larry 117
Federici, Danny 99
Feliciano, José 28
Fender 143
Fenwick, Lucy 17
Fig, Anton 99 100 104
Flugelhorn 132 134
Fly Records 17 – see Cube
Freeman, Don 152 161+

Gage, Pete Ch4 32+ 48+ 51
    57 61 113
Gambaccini, Paul 45 125+
    145 154 155 158
Garafolo, Bryan 77 81
Garay, Val 118
Garfunkel 6 87
Gate Cinema 146
Gaynor, Mel 129 130
Genesis 117
Glass, Philip 162
Golga, Eddie 142
Gottehrer, Richard Ch10 106
    113
Graham, Bill 139
Green, Derek 32+ 38 47 56
    66 98
Greetham, Steve 135+
    140+ 146 158+
Guitar 36 37 58 142 145 152
    (see also under
    Armatrading)
Guyana 8 10

Hair Ch2 7+ 11 17 76
    (photos)
Halsey, John 36
Ham, Bill 91
Hamlet 8
Hammersmith Odeon 52 63
    71+ 82 114
Harmonica 134 145
Harmonium 19
Havens, Richie 39 69
Hayward, Richie 94 103
Hendrix, Jimi 30 36 37 162
Hepworth, David 72
High Court 122 127+
Hildreth, Justin 114 121
Hirsh, Ricky 94 99 103
Holland, Bernie 39
Honkey Château 17
Hopkin, Mary 16
Horses 159
Hounds of Love 146
Howlett, Mike Ch13 157

'If' 21
Interview – see under
    Armatrading
Island records 39

Jackson, Joe 131+ 134
Jansen, Steve 161+
Jewell, Derek 25
Jewell, Jimmy 63+ 71+ 73
John, Elton 13 17 18 21 24
    149 157 158
Johns, Glyn Ch6 Ch9 23 54
    70 75 77+ 81 93 95+
    97 113 151
Johnstone, Davy 18
Jones, Kenny 49 59 (photo)

Karn, Mick 152 162
Katché, Manu 40
Katz, David 31
Katz, Robin 51 81
Kemper, Dave 77 81
Kent, Nick 75+
Keyboards 81 82 91 103 106
    108+ 117
King, Carole 154 157
King, Mark 159
Kingston, Surrey 103 113
Knopfler, Mark 144 150 152
    154 159
Knowles, Greg 50
Kongos, John 17 26

Ladies of the Canyon 21 45
Lane, Jamie 49+ 54 148+
   151+ 158 161
Laverde, Durban 49 50+ 53
Lawall, Gasper 39
Lawley, Sue 14 159
Lee, Albert 36 70 74
Leggat, Mr Justice 127+
Leibovitz, Annie 86 92 (photo)
Lennon, John 13
Levin, Tony 106 116
Lewis, Linda 28
Lewy, Henry 97
Lillywhite, Steve Ch11 Ch12
   36 129 143 162
Live Aid 139
Lock, Graham 94
Lofgren, Nils 54
Long, Janice 127
Lyle, Graham 151
Lyricon 83 87

McCartney, Paul 16
McDermott, Galt 8
McTell, Ralph 17
Magoogan, Wesley 144
Mandela, Nelson 156
Maplethorpe, Robert 133
Markee, Dave Ch6 67 77+
   83+ 86
Marley, Bob 101
Marotta, Jerry 106 117 129
Marshall, Austin John 29
Martyn, John 66
Mathewson, Ron 44
Mattacks, Dave 54 57+ 67
   70 71 77 148+
May, Chris 88
Melody Maker 7 25 26 28 43
   49 66+ 80 88 91+ 160
   (photos)
Micro Moog 108
Milligan, Spike 66
Mitchell, Joni 19 21 23 25 36
   45 67 74 86 97 110 154
Mogotsi, Pearl 7 12
Morrison, Van 25 157
Moss, Jerry 32 47
Movies Ch5 56 62 121 148
Music:
   blues 46 120 134 162+
   calypso and Latin 39 126
      154 162+
   classical 3
   country 36
   folk 23 33 38+ 44 46

funk 39
gospel 21 24 46 80 162+
heavy metal 144 162+
jazz 4 35 38+ 44 46 134
   153+
Motown 23
punk 120 135
reggae 3 25 39 85 101 107
   112 121 126
soul 3 7 33 49 120

Nashville 71
National Front 95
Nestor, Pam Ch2 Ch3 9 10+
   17 20 24 25 26 28 29
   30 34 46 54+ 65 66 70
   76 79 120 (photos)
New Musical Express 29 72 75
   94
New York 29 52 79+ 98+
   104 118 137
Newman, Tony 39
Nicoli, Fabio 47
Noble, Mike 16+ 26 53 122
   135 149+
Noel Gay Organization 12
Nunez, Pearl Mogotsi 7 12

Old Grey Whistle Test 50 73
Open Door 29
Ovation guitar 37 77

Palladino, Pino 129 130 150
   152
Palmer, Philip 83+ 121
   122+ 129 147 148+
   151 153 155+ 159
Parkinson, Michael 73
Parnell, Mark 135 141
Photographs 24 25 47 66 86
   92 102 118 120 133+
   143 155
Piano 54 89 132 154
   finger-/thumb-piano 79 82
   (see also under
   Armatrading)
Pincott, Colin 36+
Pinhorn, Maggie 30
Plytas, Nick 106 121 130
Poetry 10 21 22 65 89
Pope, Roger 17
Powell, Judy 13
Price, Lon 94
Prince 144 162
Prince's Trust 158+

Prophet 103 108 (see also
   Synthesizer)
Publishers 14 112 (see also
   Essex Music)

Q magazine 119
Quaye, Caleb 17

Radio City 137
Radio Four, Radio One – see
   BBC
Raitt, Bonny 87
Rebecca 129+
Record Mirror 81
Red Rocks 137
Reviews 25 28 51 66+ 72 80
Rhodes, David 129 130
Rock Against Racism 95
Roland 108
Rolling Stone 31
Ross, Jim 135+ 137 142+
   146+
Roussell, Jean 39
Rubyfruit Jungle 92

St Kitts 1 4 67 125+
Sanford, Gary 112
Saxophone 63 117 120 132
   135 144 145 162
Scary Monsters 112 120
Semper, June 7
Shakespeare, Robbie 40 107
   112
Shepherd, Andy 162
Sherry Copeland Artistes 28
   29 32 48
Sherry, John 26 48
Simmonds, Mike 121
Simms, Dick 83 103
Simon, Paul 6 67 87
Simone, Nina 26 154 157
Sitar 19
Small, Dag 50 52
Snowdon 143
Songs – see Armatrading,
   Joan: writing. Also Title
   Index which follows this
   section
Sounds 25 49 50 51 66 74
   (photo)
Space Invaders 109+
Spare Rib 94
Spedding, Chris 67 99 104
Spinetti, Henry 13 26 28 30
   31 77+ 83 85+
The Stage 7

Standard 145
Star Trek 92
Steele, Larry 13 17 18 26 30 40
Steele, Liza 13
Stevens, Cat 13 18 23 28
Stigwood, Robert 7
Stills, Stephen 19 73
Stone, Mike 26 31+ 38 47 48+ 51 53 122 127+
Strings 101 131
Studios:
  Basing Street 39+
  Battery 129+
  Bumpkin Ch15 128 140+ 145
  Château d'Herouville Ch3 17+
  Marquee 17 21
  Morgan 28
  Nomis 135
  Olympic 17 57+ 78 84+ 153
  Polar 116+
  PSL 67
  Record Plant 100+
  Rockfield 35+
  Stone Room 108
  Strawberry Ch3 17+

Town House 106+ 108
Trident 21 26
Sturmer, Daryl 117
Sumiko 24 25 (photo)
Sunday Times 25
Supertramp 52 54
Sutcliffe, Phil 66
Swaziland 159
Sydney 123 126 138
Synthesizer 107 134 143 161+ (see also Prophet)

Taj Mahal 79
Taupin, Bernie 20
Tel Aviv 136 137 139
Television 4 29 50 73 82 92 116 127 158
Thear, Rod 41
Thomas, Chris 93
Tin Pan Alley 12
Touring 28 29 54 69 76 94 114 116 121+ 136 146 155+
Townsend, Pete 159
Track Record video 96 121 125+ 126+
Tracks 143
Trench, Fiacra 131
Trumpet 117 132 135 153

Tuesday Productions 17 25 31
Tunde's Film 30

Ure, Midge 156
USA 29 32 52 54 69+ 76 81 121+ 136 137 146

Valentine, Penny 25 45 50 88 91+
Vinegar Joe 32

Wallis, Mark 141
Wayne, John 65
Welch, Chris 28
Wembley Arena 95
Wembley Stadium 156
West Indies 1 101 (see also St Kitts)
'What A Piece of Work Is Man' 8
White, Alex 135 140 146+
Whitehead, Annie 117
The Wild Geese 89+
Williams, Richard 50 67
Wong, Kimi 8 9 (photos)

York, Steve 36
Young, Red 81 82 89 91 94

Title Index

(The first page number listed is usually the main entry)

Alice 24 73
All A Woman Needs 154
All The Kings' Gardens 12 16 23 26
All The Way From America 103 100
Always 162 +
Am I Blue For You 88
Angelman 144
At The Hop 112

Baby I 88
Back To The Night Ch4 49 50 56 69 70 75 129 163
Back To The Night 29 74 82
Bad Habits 120
Barefoot and Pregnant 87 92
Body To Dust 44 45
Bottom To The Top 85 +

Call Me Names 119 118 158
Can't Let Go 161 +
Child Star 19 21 23 158
City Girl 23
Come When You Need Me 45 46
Cool Blue Stole My Heart 70 82 95 112

Dark Truths 154
The Dealer 120
The Devil I Know 153
Did I Make You Up 152 154

Don Juan 144 +
Down To Zero 63 58 59 62 73 82
Drop the Pilot 118 120 126 127
Dry Land 41 45 46 52 54 70 74 154

Eating The Bear 112 + 109
Everybody Gotta Know 120 144

Feeling In My Heart 101 102
Figure Of Speech 144
Flight Of The Wild Geese 89 + 96
Foolish Pride 120
Free 162 +
Friends 102
Frustration 126

Game of Love 120
Gave it a Try 22
Get In The Sun 91
Get In Touch With Jesus 45 154
Good Times 162 +

Head Of The Table 22 23
Hearts and Flowers 152 158 161 +
Hearts and Flowers 161 +
Heaven 126

Help Yourself 59
How Cruel 96 97

I Can't Lie To Myself 107 112
I Love My Baby 118 120
I'm Lucky 108 109 112 126
I Need You 101 102
It Could Have Been Better 23 102 158
I Wanna Hold You 112

Jesse 144 145
Joan Armatrading Ch6 Ch7 23 53 82 91 148 154 155 157
Join The Boys 59 64 70

The Key Ch12 29 134 144
The Key 120
Killing Time 143
Kind Words 143 146
Kissin' And A Huggin' 80 96

Laurel And The Rose 144 143 145
Let It Last 89
Like Fire 65
Live At The Bijou Club 70 +
Living For You 151 + 153 158
Lonely Lady 28 96
Love And Affection 65 52 + 57 62 64 69 70 73 74

91 96 121 126 131 133
156 160 161
Love By You 131 134
Love Song 96

Mama Mercy 79 91 95
Ma-Me-O-Beach 102
Mean Old Man 22 23 24 162
Me Myself I Ch10 112 121
Me Myself I 103 126
More Than One Kind Of Love
161+
Moves 134
My Family 21 12 14 19 22
23 24

Never Is Too Late 79
No Love 104 110 112
No Love For Free 44

One More Chance 144 145
One Night 135
Only One 110 113
Opportunity 78 79 82

Peace In Mind 80
People 64 68
Persona Grata 131 134
The Power of Dreams 162+
Promise Land 162+

Reach Out 144
Romancers 112
Rosie 96+ 126

Save Me 65 68
Secret Secrets Ch13 140
Secret Secrets 135
The Shouting Stage Ch15 144
The Shouting Stage 154
Show Some Emotion Ch8 91
Show Some Emotion 79 23 70
92 101 117 126
Simon 102+ 101 154
Sleight of Hand Ch14 139 158
So Good 40
Somebody Who Loves You 65
Someone's In The Background
162+
Something In The Air Tonight
162+
Spend A Little Time 24 26
Steppin' Out 95+
Steppin' Out 45 46 70 74 82
96 126
Straight Talk 154
Strange 135
Stronger Love 154 158

Taking My Baby Up Town 88
80 94 154
Talking To The Wall 132 134
Tall In The Saddle 53 65 71
82 96
Tell Tale 116 117 120
Temptation 134
To the Limit Ch9 91 101 121
148
Together in Words and Music
28

Track Record 127 121
Travel So Far 45
Turn Out The Light 100 102

Visionary Mountains 22 19
23 24

Walk Under Ladders Ch11 117
118 120 121 129 144
Warm Love 79
Watch Your Step 154
Water With The Wine 68 53
59 71
The Weakness In Me 112 127
What Do Boys Dream 118
120 127
What Do You Want 89
Whatever's For Us Ch3 14 21
24+ 46 73 87 102
Whatever's For Us 19
When I Get It Right 112 127
154
When You Kisses Me 99
Willow 77 80 82 114 123
126 136 144
Wishing 89
Words 154
Woncha Come On Home 79
82 154

Your Letter 87 92
You Rope You Tie Me 87 88
96